# Park Synagogue    MARCH 2000

Presented By:
CYNTHIA CARSON & SONS

In Memory Of:
KENNETH CARSON

# VISITING the SICK

# VISITING the SICK
## The Mitzvah of Bikur Cholim

### SHARON SELIB EPSTEIN

JASON ARONSON INC.
*Northvale, New Jersey*
*Jerusalem*

This book was set in 11 pt. Goudy by Hightech Data Inc., of Bangalore, India, and printed and bound by Book-mart Press, Inc. of North Bergen, NJ.

**Library of Congress Cataloging-in-Publication Data**

Epstein, Sharon Selib, 1947–
    Visiting the sick : the mitzvah of bikur cholim / by Sharon Selib
  Epstein.
        p.  cm.
    Includes bibliographical references and index.
    ISBN 0-7657-6075-4 (alk. paper)
    1. Visiting the sick (Judaism) I. Title.
  BM729.V5E77   1999
  296.3'6—dc21                                          98-51751

Printed in the United States of America on acid-free paper. For information and catalog write to Jason Aronson Inc., 230 Livingston Street, Northvale, NJ 07647-1726, or visit our website: www.aronson.com

# DEDICATION

This book is dedicated to my parents, the late Morris Selib and the late Goldie Goldman Selib, both of blessed memory, who taught me from a young age about the importance of being there for people in failing health.

I also dedicate this book to my brother Harvey Selib and sister Judith Marshall, who both served as role models as we were growing up, and to my Bubby, Fannie Selib, whose many stories about how it was "back when" kindled my respect and love for the aged.

I dedicate this book also to my late in-laws Frederick Epstein and Lillian Scheinert Epstein, both of blessed memory, and to my brother-in-law Richard Epstein. My mother-in-law lived at home, with the help of nursing aid and Richard's supervision and loving care, prior to her death from cancer. Her excitement and great outpourings of joy, in spite of her failing health, when we brought her grandchildren to visit are proof of the importance of *bikur cholim*. She rallied from their presence. Richard's strength and courage allowed her to live at home as she was dying.

I dedicate this book to our four children—Michael, Elana, Rachel, and Lisa. They are very understanding every Sunday afternoon when I disappear for three hours to go to the Long Island State Veteran's Home to perform *bikur cholim*. Every Christmas when our synagogue goes to Stony Brook University Hospital, the girls join me willingly for *bikur cholim*, and they go to a variety of local nursing homes with their youth group. They also came to the *bikur cholim* training that I helped organize for Suffolk Jewish Communal Planning Council and that was given by Rabbi Isaac Trainin and his staff.

Finally, but most important, to my husband, Larry, I dedicate this book to you. Without your inspiration, this book would not exist. You encouraged me to write about what is important to me.

# CONTENTS

ACKNOWLEDGMENTS     vii

INTRODUCTION     xiii

*BIKUR CHOLIM*: SOME TRUE STORIES     1

*BIKUR CHOLIM* IN JEWISH THOUGHT AND HISTORY     11

ILLNESS, DEATH, AND DYING     17

COMMON FEARS ABOUT VISITING THE SICK:
WHY PEOPLE DON'T VISIT     33

AFTER THE DECISION: STEPS TO TAKE IN VISITING
THE SICK     43

DEVELOPING *BIKUR CHOLIM* SKILLS     55

HOW TO START A *BIKUR CHOLIM* COMMITTEE     103

EFFECTIVE VOLUNTEER PROGRAMS     147

# Contents

RESOURCE GUIDE     165

READING GUIDE     169

INDEX     175

# ACKNOWLEDGMENTS

This book exists because of the influences of so many people in my life. The seed was planted in my childhood by my family. My late father, Morris Selib, courageously suffered through many illnesses when I was a child. He and my late mother, Goldie Selib, and my brother and sister, Harvey Selib and Judith Selib Marshall, taught me the values of compassion and of being there to visit the sick. I also thank my late aunt, my father's sister Jeanette Weiss, for teaching me patience during my father's illness.

The late Rabbi Isaac Klein, my synagogue rabbi from childhood through my marriage, provided spiritual comfort to our family during the period when my father died and afterward.

Through my teenage years, after my father's death, there were *bikur cholim* visits to Bubby Fannie Selib in her nursing home and her joyful cries of "You saved my life" (*Lebense*, in Yiddish) every time we came.

These roots of *bikur cholim* lay dormant in me until my late mother-in-law Lillian Scheinert Epstein's fatal illness. She was a courageous woman, knowing that she had lived for fourteen years beyond, according to her doctors, her allotted time. She was able to see the birth of her four grandchildren and a good part of their childhoods. She appreciated the time she had left and proved to us the importance of *bikur cholim*, as she excitedly greeted her grandchildren when they came to visit her in her dying days. One month after her death I knew it was time for me to make a regular commitment to perform *bikur cholim*, and I still do so in tribute to my father and my mother-in-law.

In my volunteer experience I owe thanks especially to Anita Risener, a social worker at Stony Brook University Hospital who was in charge of the ALC (Alternate Level of Care) Program, which worked with long-term patients who were either waiting for nursing home placements or who had medical problems so severe that there might not be any other kind of placement for them. I thank Anita for matching me up with patients who had few visitors and perhaps needed them most. My greatest challenges resulted in my greatest fulfillment through this program. I also thank the late Laurence Goldstein, the critically ill patient in his nineties whom I visited weekly for over two years until his death. He helped me come to terms with the death of my father nearly thirty years earlier.

In my volunteer work at the Long Island State Veterans Home, I would like to thank Father Charles Kohli, a true role model for how to perform *bikur cholim*. His interactions with patients of all faiths show genuine caring and compassion. He uses humor in dealing with patients and volunteers. I'll never forget the time he told the part-time rabbi at the home that I was a saint.

At the Veterans Home I have numerous friends to thank. These include: the late Humbert Monaco, who lived almost to his 101st birthday and who enthusiastically filled me in firsthand on the history of his life prior to World War I and onward. Fred Goldstein, an active resident who sings, writes, and participates in many other activities too numerous to list, is one of my Scrabble friends. My challenge in life is to win a game. Eighty-seven-year-old Anna Clark, my Scrabble pal, gives me exciting stories about World War II and the Eisenhower administration, of which she was an active part. She helps me understand the theme of the "I like Ike" buttons that I vaguely remember during his political campaign when I was a young child.

I thank Judith Shivak from North Shore Jewish Center, our synagogue. Every year she organizes family visits on Christmas to Stony Brook University Hospital. It is one of the most successful *bikur cholim* programs our synagogue has, and it is very important because once a year it gives families an experience in *bikur cholim*. There have not been any studies conducted to see whether it results in recruiting long-term volunteers, but it does make parents role models for a very positive activity.

I also must thank Arthur Kurzweil, vice president of Jason Aronson Inc., for his support of this effort. Arthur has been a true friend to my family and his caring soul understood the need for a book on *bikur cholim*.

I have many rabbis whom I also would like to thank. To Rabbi Howard Hoffman, my congregational rabbi, I thank you for working so hard in the community to set up the pastoral counseling course, which I attended for eight weeks and which resulted in introducing me to the Long Island State Veteran's Home. I also thank you for your help in setting up and actively participating in our synagogue training on *bikur cholim*.

To Rabbi Adam Fisher, a true believer in *bikur cholim*, I appreciated your *bikur cholim* visit during my twelve-day hospitalization in 1990. Your prayer was my connection to the Jewish community. Your innovative healing service that I attended recently shows your continued interest and caring for people's well-being.

To Rabbi Steven Moss, who has mastered the art of *bikur cholim* over the years as a rabbi. I appreciate the way you try to get lay members of the Jewish community involved, too. I appreciate that as president of the Suffolk Jewish Communal Planning Council, you supported and were very active in getting the Jewish Community involved in a *bikur cholim* training that the council sponsored. Thanks here also go to Susan Lustig, executive director of the Suffolk Jewish Communal Planning Council, who took on more than her share of work in order to allow this county *bikur cholim* training to come to fruition.

To Rabbi Isaac Trainin, executive vice president of the Coordinating Council of Bikur Cholim of Greater New York, I thank
you for your involvement and for offering training to synagogues
and organizations in the New York City area. Your experience
and expertise provided us with very inspiring training from the
Suffolk Jewish Planning Council.

To Rabbi Bradley Shavit Artson, thanks for your advice and
contact via e-mail.

To Rabbi Eugene Borowitz, I thank you for allowing me to
share my feelings on *bikur cholim* in an issue of *Sh'ma* devoted to
experiences with issues of death and dying. This, and a later publication in *Na'Amat Woman* on "Visiting The Sick," helped encourage me to take the step of writing a book. I thank Judith
Sokoloff, the editor, for the opportunity to publish and the encouragement to write.

I also thank the late Viktor Frankl. His book *Man's Search for
Meaning* has been one of the key influences in my life. It helped
me see and understand that *bikur cholim* at this time has become
my mission in life. At first, it was enough to visit patients in the
hospital on a weekly basis, but as I've grown, I've learned that
the actions I must take in my mission must grow, too. It was a
process of experience and growth that allowed me to take this step
at this time and not before. I thank Dr. Frankl because I sent him
a letter explaining my interest in *bikur cholim* and inquiring about
any logotherapy courses that might be available in a nearby area.
His reply to my letter encouraged me to just continue with the
work I was doing, that my actions were going in the right direction.

In doing research for the book, I had mail and phone contact
with many helpful people. I especially want to thank Susie Kessler
from the National Center For Jewish Healing for suggesting many
important resources and for sending me reading material. I also
thank Janet Peshek, executive assistant at the Harry and Jeanette
Weinberg Jewish Terrace, who read my article in *Na'Amat Woman*
and contacted me about *bikur cholim* and made me aware of her
agency program. Also, I thank Kristin Mathisen, community re-

lations director at the Weinberg Jewish Terrace, for the interview and carefully researched written materials. At the Rosalind and Joseph Gurwin Jewish Geriatric Center, I thank Herb Friedman, the dedicated executive director, for the on-site meeting session and tour of the home for the Suffolk Jewish Communal Planning Council, and I thank Kathleen Donnelly, director of volunteers at Gurwin for her in-depth tour and interview on the workings of the volunteer program.

My most important thanks go to friends and family. My college friend Mary Day Brown Barez gave me the courage to try something new, to dream what might seem to be the impossible and then to pursue it. My childhood friend Donna Paxson and her mother, Doris, remind me that the need for *bikur cholim* is ever present, as I speak with Donna about her daily dedication to her elderly mother, who can no longer live alone unsupervised in her own home. My admiration goes to Mary Lee Elias, my friend for nearly thirty years, who courageously lives her life from day to day with a rare lung disease for which there is no cure. I thank my four children: Michael, Elana, Rachel, and Lisa. It is with enormous satisfaction that I watch your actions and note how much they emulate the principles of caring and compassion. Yes, Lisa, your volunteer work at the soup kitchen is very important, and it is with great pride that I tell people about the day Lisa and Rachel participated in building a house in the Habitat for Humanity Program and about Elana's volunteer work in the Special Olympics.

Most of all, I thank my husband, Larry, who dared to plant the seed in my mind that writing a book was the next step I needed to make in order to grow in pursuing my mission. You dared to suggest it before I could accept the responsibility of what needed to be done. Without your patience and guidance there would be no book.

# INTRODUCTION

As a young child in Hebrew school I remember learning the term *mitzvah* to mean a good deed. It was an act of kindness that I should perform, and after doing it I would feel good about myself. This was also reinforced by the praise I received from my parents and anyone else who witnessed my actions, especially when I did such things as visit the old lady who lived upstairs.

As I grew older, I began to learn the true meaning of a *mitzvah* through my own life experiences. For me, my father's series of heart attacks and strokes while I was growing up and his untimely death when I was fourteen provided my first memory of performing *bikur cholim*, the *mitzvah* of visiting the sick. My parents had always tried to shelter me from what they perceived to be pain unfit for a child. A child should not have to witness dying. But they were unable to hide the six years of suffering that my father experienced as his health began to fail. They never spoke openly about his impending death, but I sensed it. Many nights I would awaken in the middle of the night just to listen. I was relieved to hear his snoring. That was my reassurance that he was still alive and breathing.

I have vivid memories of my father's stroke when I was twelve years old. It affected his motor coordination on his right side. He used to have petite, readable handwriting that looked almost like a piece of artwork. As a result of this stroke, he could never produce this type of art again. He was determined and spent a lot of time practicing and asking for our approval, just as a three-year-old who is learning to print for the first time asks his parents and teachers for approval. His closest rendition of his name, which was Morris, looked something like "Miky." When he asked for my approval, I told him it was good and walked away—devastated. I didn't dare ask my mother if he was going to get better. I was much too afraid to hear the answer.

When I was fourteen, my father had another heart attack, and he was hospitalized and placed in an oxygen tent. He went into a coma and did not respond to any of us. Our family camped out in the hospital waiting room, and no one spoke of his impending death. It was painful for me to see him in this condition, and I did not have to visit him in his room. But in reality I did have to see him, and I made periodic trips into his room to observe the situation. There was a deeper pull within me that compelled me to visit my father in the hospital as he lay dying in a coma in an oxygen tent. I don't remember whether I talked to him or held his hand, but I knew I had to be there. I would take periodic trips from the safety of the waiting room into his room to listen to the sounds of his impending death.

After my father's death, I did occasional volunteer work in hospitals until my life became shaped by additional experiences that validated *bikur cholim* and gave it true meaning in my life. It took thirty years for me to come to terms with my father's untimely death, and I am convinced that for me, this was achieved by my visiting dying patients in the hospital, holding their hands, and giving them the human contact that other people too often shy away from.

My own hospitalization for the removal of a brain tumor on February 1, 1990, was an especially important stepping-stone in my life that helped me experience firsthand the need for *bikur cholim.* I had denied the symptoms of my illness for three years, had made excuses for the leg pains that prevented me from walking at a normal pace, and had compensated for short-term memory loss (which was easily done when my family physician continually attributed it to middle-aged memory loss). My husband realized the seriousness of my memory loss while preparing for our son's *Bar Mitzvah*: the people from whom we had ordered decorations finally got in contact with us after they realized that the phone number I had given them was incorrect. The phone number I had given them, minus the area code, was for the home in which I had grown up in Buffalo, New York, from age nine. I returned to my family physician, and he agreed to give me a referral for an evaluation. I was so sure that the referral would be to a psychiatrist that a sigh of relief passed over me as he gave me the name of a neurologist who was the head of a local hospital neurology department. The neurology appointment and two ensuing MRI evaluations resulted in the discovery of a brain tumor and a twelve-day hospitalization to remove it.

Even though my family visited daily, I was extremely lonely. I was desperate for human contact other than the nurses who came in four times each day to take vital statistics. When a stranger— a seminary student of a different religion than my own—knocked on the door to ask if he could speak to me, I welcomed him into my room. I spoke with other patients in the halls and listened to their war stories, recognizing the hunger for human contact we all were desperately seeking. Even my own former congregation rabbi, for whatever reason, never made any direct contact with me during the twelve days I was hospitalized for surgery and recuperation. Apparently, this is not an uncommon experience. When I sought information from readers of Jewish publications about their experiences with *bikur cholim,* one man wrote to tell me how hurt he felt about being hospitalized twice in three years and having no rabbi or representative of his congregation even call to inquire about his health. He was devastated because it seemed to him that no one cared.

One year after my hospitalization, my next stepping-stone toward understanding the importance of *bikur cholim* occurred. My mother-in-law had experienced a mastectomy six months prior to the birth of my first child, her first grandchild. Her surgeon gave her six months to live. She wanted grandchildren so much that she refused to give up and lived a relatively healthy life for fourteen more years, thus being able to enjoy her grandson and his three sisters, who were born within a seven-year period. The cancer returned, and even my mother-in-law realized its impact and began preparing herself for her impending death. Her welcoming smiles whenever I came to visit her at home as she lay slowly dying, and her bursts of energy as she stretched out her arms to welcome her grandchildren when we brought them to her for short visits, all helped me understand the value and the need for *bikur cholim*.

A newborn baby goes through trauma as it leaves the safety of its mother's womb, and it is welcomed into this world. So, too, have I been able to understand that our sick and dying need not to feel deserted in their difficult and final days.

A book I read by Viktor Frankl, titled *Man's Search for Meaning*, has also helped me understand the meaning of *bikur cholim*. Frankl, a neurologist and a psychiatrist, spent three years at Auschwitz, Dachau, and other concentration camps during World War II. Part of the reason he survived these adverse conditions was because of his inner goals. He needed to be alive to be reunited with any of his family members who might survive the concentration camps. He needed to live in order to complete a book he had begun to write before being imprisoned.

For me, *bikur cholim* has become a mission in life. It started as a good deed but has transcended that, as my life experiences and my maturity allowed me to perform *bikur cholim* at different levels at my own pace. I'm embarrassed when patients I visit compliment me for my actions. Because it is a mission in my life, I feel that *bikur cholim* validates my life. Sometimes I feel a fleeting inner warmth as I experience *bikur cholim* within my soul. Frankl describes this inner warmth in his book as something that gives meaning to one's life; *bikur cholim* is more than simply a *mitzvah*.

I was very excited when I read in my synagogue bulletin that an interfaith training workshop would be held at a local hospital for eight weeks and that those interested could obtain an application. I benefited greatly from this seminar, which was run by eight clergy people, but I wondered why there were only two out of thirty-three participants who were from the Jewish faith. Clearly, the vital *mitzvah* of *bikur cholim*, once so valued and so widely practiced within the Jewish community, needed to be revived.

I have been volunteering weekly at a local hospital since February 1991 and at a local nursing home since June 1993. Many of the people I have visited have been long term patients. Some await nursing home placements. Others have died before any placements could be made. Even as they lay dying, I have come to understand the importance of human contact for them, and I have gained from my associations with them.

The world has changed since my childhood. The elderly population has increased as technology, treatment, and life-sustaining devices have improved. Now, more than ever, the need for *bikur cholim* exists.

I am writing this book because I recognize the importance of introducing *bikur cholim* to everyone at a level that is comfortable for the individual.

A survey that I did in 1994 for the Suffolk Jewish Communal Planning Council (on Long Island, New York) indicated that many synagogues did not have formal *bikur cholim* committees but were interested in exploring training programs. Some synagogue officers expressed pessimism that the training sessions might not be well attended because people might be too busy with other aspects of their lives and might not feel able to fit *bikur cholim* into their schedules. Others have given excuses that although *bikur cholim* is a good deed, they do not feel comfortable doing it.

In April 1995 Rabbi Isaac Trainin, executive vice president of the Coordinating Council on Bikur Cholim, presented a training seminar in Suffolk County, which we organized through the Suffolk Jewish Communal Planning Council. We invited rabbis, synagogue members, and nursing home and hospital personnel. The turnout was approximately fifty people. This appears to be a clear indication that people are not choosing to try *bikur cholim*. This conclusion was reinforced when in April 1996, I presented a three-week training seminar on *Bikur* Cholim to our six hundred-member synagogue. One woman called to ask if her ten-year-old daughter could become involved in this training and offered to drop the child off for the sessions and pick her up. The mother herself would not be staying for the training. Only five people came to the program, and three were already involved in some kind of volunteer activity for *bikur cholim*.

This book, if it succeeds, will supplement existing efforts, to ignite renewed interest in the *mitzvah* of *bikur cholim*.

I begin the book with a discussion of the importance of *bikur cholim* and then discuss *bikur cholim* in Jewish religious literature. Next, I describe *bikur cholim* activities that are being undertaken in the Jewish community. I talk about psychological aspects of visiting the sick and the fears and excuses people use to avoid performing this *mitzvah*. Next, I deal with step-by-step methods of learning how to visit the sick. Finally, I introduce ideas about how institutions such as synagogues can plan *bikur cholim* activities.

In the pastoral counseling course that I took at a local hospital, a Protestant pastor suggested that pastoral care is rooted in Psalms 23. I found this to be a meaningful image for my link to previous and future generations and our link to God. God is our Shepherd, and He guides and teaches us. God knows us and our need to go in the direction of righteousness. We learn to participate, to fulfill our lives individually. However, we move through life not just as individuals but also as part of a community. As members of the Jewish community, who are responsible for one another and fully dedicated to this idea of *Klal Yisrael*, we must help ourselves and each other survive and find meaning in our lives.

# CHAPTER ONE

# *BIKUR CHOLIM*: SOME TRUE STORIES

Laurence G. was ninety-four when I was first introduced to him. He had been hospitalized for three years. Each breath he took was aided by a ventilator. His body was paralyzed, but his mind was alert, and he could communicate by mouthing words.

I was very nervous the first few times I visited. When he coughed, I was sure I was about to witness a death, and it scared me. In the beginning I found myself feeling obligated to perform a monologue, and I felt tongue-tied after I told him my name, age, marital status, and the names and ages of my children. There was only one additional variable that changed from week to week, and that was "the weather." I tried to ask him a few questions, but I felt embarrassed when he answered and I was unable to interpret what he was saying. When I asked him to repeat the answers, it posed the same problem because I still did not understand him.

Something drew me to continue visiting weekly in spite of these hardships. Perhaps it was the smile he flashed when I came into the room. We developed a routine to our relationship; he had company to help him through the loneliness of his day. He was able

1

to communicate his desires to me. I would rub his neck, comb his hair, and read to him.

His family visited once or twice a week, but it was hard for his eighty-year-old wife and his eighty-eight-year-old "kid brother" to come often and stay long. The days must have been long and boring. Often I had to wear a mask, gloves, and a gown to go into the room because he had an infection. Too often, he did not get visitors. It was much easier for workers or potential visitors to pass him by, either because it was too much trouble to dress for the occasion or because they assumed what I had assumed the day his social worker introduced me to him. How does one communicate with someone who cannot verbalize his thoughts and needs? Would there be any benefit for him to have a visitor when there was no verbal communication? I found out the answers to these questions, and I benefited greatly from my visits to him. He taught me a lot about life and helped me cope with issues in my past that I had not dealt with for many years—the death of my father, in particular.

One day his family left a story he had written, to be read at a dinner where he was being honored for seventy-five years as a volunteer at a local fire department in his hometown. The story began with an incident describing how he had lied about his age when he was sixteen so that he could become a member of the newly formed fire department, in which the age requirement was eighteen or older. His father was one of the founders, and he wanted to be a part of the action. Every time I visited him, he would ask me to read this story, and I always looked forward to it. I came to understand this ninety-four-year-old paralyzed man as a young mischievous lad who performed the kind of pranks that I did as a child and the kind of pranks my own children still try on me. Maybe the times have changed. Technology has advanced, but people still have the same basic instincts. I got to know this man through his story.

As I was rubbing his neck and combing his hair, I frequently thought about the father I had lost when I was in my teens. I feel that through Laurence G., who was only a few years older than my father would have been had he lived, I was able to honor my father in a way I could not while my father was sick and dying.

Notes that were left on Laurence's bulletin board from his family indicated that he had communicated to them that he enjoyed our time together. I never considered our visits to be a good deed. My personal gains were so much more than just a *mitzvah*. Even though Laurence died three years ago, the impact his life had on mine will never fade. He taught me the true meaning of life.

Taking care of Laurence G. is an example of an ancient Jewish *mitzvah*, or religious commandment, called *bikur cholim*.

*Bikur cholim* literally means "visiting the sick," although the concept has wider meanings as well. Not only does it refer to going to where sick people reside, whether in private homes, nursing homes, or hospitals, but it also includes other activities to make those who are ill or dying feel more comforted and comfortable.

According to Rabbi Isaac Trainin, executive vice president of the Coordinating Council on Bikur Cholim, " . . . the word *bikur* actually means 'examination.' It is our religious obligation not only to visit the sick in hospitals and in nursing homes and the homebound, but to determine in what other ways we may be of help." For a fuller understanding of Rabbi Trainin's views, readers can get the training manual published by the Coordinating Council on Bikur Cholim of Greater New York, which will be discussed in greater detail later on.

The story of Laurence G. illustrates what most people typically have in mind to be *bikur cholim*, and many feel it is not something they can handle. But, as Rabbi Trainin indicates, *bikur cholim* can include a variety of other activities as well. Besides helping the sick and elderly cope with new roles that are seemingly beyond their control, *bikur cholim* volunteers can help family members cope with their feelings concerning someone's illness and/or frailty. Volunteers can help children with role reversals they may now have to accept, as they are forced into becoming caretakers for their parents and grandparents; can help the sick and elderly cope with the loss of support of the Jewish community, as they find themselves unable to go to the synagogue for

Jewish holidays and celebrations; and can help people understand and cope with natural stages in the life cycle.

Ninety-eight-year-old Albert was in a nursing home for five years prior to his death. He told his volunteer visitor chilling stories about actively fighting in World War I. Twice, he narrowly escaped death. He married and had five children. One of his sons were already deceased from heart disease and another had died from kidney failure at the time the volunteer had known Albert for over a year. Albert's health was relatively good, and he had trouble handling the fact that his sons had to suffer while he was physically healthy.

Albert's volunteer listened to his complaints about his frustrations and his pains, including a story about the death of his wife twenty-five years earlier from a sudden heart attack. As he talked about these ordeals, he intertwined the stories with details about his own active life. For example, at age eighty-six he climbed on the roof of his Queens home to fix the TV antenna. The volunteer, by listening to Albert's stories, became acquainted with the real Albert: the young child who had been very devoted to his mother and who had fought with his younger brother for being disrespectful to her; to Albert as a young man, who had many girlfriends when he was growing up but who pursued his wife and ignored the other girls when they tried to win his affection.

As Albert found a friend in his volunteer, he became less frustrated and began to give advice about the hardships in life and how to survive them. He could no longer climb up to his roof to fix his TV antenna, but now he had developed a new expertise. He could give advice on how to survive.

Albert's volunteer helped him deal with the frailties of old age by allowing him to feel the importance of telling his own story. Albert benefited, as is shown by his jealousy when his volunteer paid attention to other residents.

One woman became a *bikur cholim* volunteer without even realizing that she was doing so. When her synagogue Sisterhood asked for volunteers to visit congregants in the hospital, she ignored the request. She commented to a friend that she could not handle being around sick people. She would be too uncomfortable seeing others suffer and knowing that she had no power to take away their illness. She admired people who could visit and comfort the ill. When she received a call from a Sisterhood member, asking if she could cook a meal that would be delivered to a frail elderly shut-in and her husband, however, she readily agreed to do this; and when she was informed how much the the recipients appreciated it, she agreed to cook them a meal each week. She had done this for two months, when the recipients asked for her phone number and called to thank her personally. The volunteer received so much pleasure from the phone call that she asked the elderly couple if she could call them periodically to inquire about their health and other needs.

The volunteer thus went at her own pace and her own level of comfort in getting involved. After several months of phone contacts and several invitations from the recipients, the volunteer nervously agreed to deliver her own home-cooked meal directly to the couple. For approximately one year the *bikur cholim* volunteer has been taking an action she never thought herself capable of. She still states firmly that at this time, hospital visits are not something she can handle, but she is not as firm now about saying she will never do them.

As is shown from this example, merely by cooking one meal and donating it to an elderly shut-in couple, one can perform *bikur cholim*. One can help an elderly couple cope with increasing frailty and loss of the ability to perform the roles they had in the past.

Families with a critically ill child could gain a lot from a *bikur cholim* visitor. The volunteer could come to the home and provide services that the parents are unable to provide because they feel an obligation to be in the hospital with their critically ill child. Two members of a volunteer group interviewed the parents of four-year-old Jennifer, who was hospitalized with brain cancer. The child's parents were grief-stricken because it appeared, from what the oncologist said, that there was limited hope for Jennifer's recovery. Jennifer's mother cried a lot as she tried to understand what was happening. Why did it have to happen to her child, who had done nothing to deserve to die?

The *bikur cholim* volunteer was there to listen to the mother's story and to allow her to talk about her feelings, but the volunteer also heard another need being expressed. That involved how the rest of the family at home was coping. Jennifer's six-year-old sister and eight-year-old brother were at home and were being cared for by their maternal grandmother. This put a lot of stress on them. The volunteer was able to assess some of this family's needs and to work out plans to take the grandmother food shopping, prepare some meals for the family, and transport the son to his weekly Cub Scout meeting and the daughter to her ballet lesson. These kinds of *bikur cholim* services eased some of the tensions that Jennifer's parents were experiencing. Also, other *bikur cholim* volunteers visited Jennifer at the hospital and read her stories and provided her with craft activities. This occasionally gave the parents time to meet some of their other needs.

Jane's mother had Alzheimer's disease. After caring for her mother for nearly a year at home, Jane decided to seek nursing home care because she felt incapable of being on twenty-four-hour-watch to be certain her mother would not wander away and/or put herself in danger by lighting a fire or walking outside in the street without looking for oncoming cars. Jane felt guilty for exploring nursing home placement. Her mother had raised her and her two sisters and always had seemed to sacrifice for her children. She was there each day when they came home from school, waiting to hear their news of the day. If they were sick, their mother was there to comfort them. Jane felt she would be a traitor if she deserted her mother in time of need.

A local Alzheimer's agency had weekly support groups for children who were now to be caretakers for their parents. Jane was encouraged to attend, but she could not leave her mother until she had been hooked up with a volunteer who was able to come to her home for a couple of hours each week. It still took several months before Jane got to a support meeting. For the first month she stayed home with the volunteer. She stated that it was im-

6

portant to be certain that her mother would accept having a stranger there. The volunteer could see that Jane was overwhelmed with guilt because she was having difficulty caring for her mother and because she was having thoughts about sending her mother away to a nursing home. The volunteer originally came with the intention of relieving Jane for a few hours so that Jane could attend support groups and/or just get out and away from the situation. Ultimately, that was accomplished, but the *bikur cholim* volunteer did more than that. She became a support for Jane at first, and then when Jane was able to trust her, she was also allowed to become a caretaker for Jane's mother for a few hours.

After nine months, Jane was finally able to move her mother into a nursing home. The volunteer comes to visit Jane's mother on a regular weekly basis now and also visits or talks to Jane at least once a month, to help Jane accept herself as a good protector who has done what she could to keep her mother safe.

I conducted a survey on all of the nursing homes in Suffolk County, Long Island, in April 1993, in which I asked each home about the number of their Jewish residents and about whether they had any regular Jewish volunteers. I learned that the volunteer directors of nearly all the homes, including homes in which there were only one or two Jewish residents, felt that Jewish residents benefited significantly from visits from Jewish volunteers. One non-Jewish volunteer director indicated that when it was time for the Jewish holidays, she would read up on ways to celebrate these holidays and would present materials to Jewish residents. Another director indicated that for the High Holidays, she would borrow a video made in 1989 from a local synagogue, and that this video would also be shared with several other local nursing homes.

One synagogue that did not have any regular weekly *bikur cholim* volunteers got together a group of a dozen volunteers to go to a local nursing home to sing Jewish songs with the residents. They were informed ahead of time that one patient, Ruth D., lived in the past and rarely spoke to anyone, and if she did, it was very difficult to understand what she was saying. Most of the volunteers said hello to her, and she ignored them. One Yiddish song that the group sang was apparently very familiar to Ruth. Suddenly, in the middle of their rendition she sang along with them in a sweet, melodious voice. Everyone was surprised. Although Ruth was unable to relate to very much that happened in the present, she had memories of the past, which, when triggered by a visit from a *bikur cholim* group, helped her relate her past to the present.

In this situation the volunteers were not comfortable doing one-on-one visiting, but they were able to present a one-time holiday program. Some of the *bikur cholim* volunteers were families with teens and young children, who participated in this form of *bikur cholim* along with their parents. One eight-year-old girl received a lot of attention from residents because they related to her as they did to their own grandchildren; she asked her parents as they were leaving if she could come back again tomorrow.

Another form of *bikur cholim* is performed almost weekly by one family, which picks up an elderly Jewish man in their neighborhood and transports him to Saturday morning services at their synagogue. The man gets reconnected to his Jewish heritage, from which he had felt cut off due to lack of transportation, but something else happens as well. The family becomes enriched, too. Sometimes they also invite the man to their home for a *Shabbat* meal after the services. He often shares stories of how *Shabbat* was celebrated when he was a child. The family members often talk about how they are able to learn Jewish history and culture firsthand from someone who lived through it. The children ask a lot of questions and often remark on how much more interesting it is for them to learn through real stories rather than through reading the material in a Hebrew school textbook.

One person explained that volunteering helped her to understand her life better and to accept that life has many stages and that each of these stages can be fulfilling. The volunteer was fifty and had just sent her fifth child away to college this year. She did not expect to feel "the empty nest syndrome" because she had been working full-time outside the home for the past ten years. Two of the older children were married, and one was expecting a child in three months, which would be her first grandchild. The volunteer had been visiting Eva, an eighty-eight-year-old woman in a nursing home, once a week for the past two years and had been playing games of Scrabble with this woman. Eva looked forward to the games and indicated that these games and her daily reading at the library kept her young and alert. If the volunteer took up some of her Scrabble time by paying attention to another resident, Eva became jealous and angry. Eva, on the other hand, was most content when she learned a new word or coaxed a new friend into joining the Scrabble game, which she defined as her panacea for the frailty of old age. Volunteers were Eva's only visitors. Her siblings, of which four out of eight were still alive, lived several hundred miles away and rarely were able to visit, but they did phone her once a week. Her two children were married, and both lived about one thousand miles away.

The volunteer's weekly talks with Eva helped her cope with the departure of her children. Eva spoke fondly about her days as a full-time parent who had never worked outside the home. After her children left home, she followed their accomplishments with great pride. She felt that she and her husband had given their children the skills and the values to help them accomplish their goals in life, and Eva learned to see their accomplishments as her achievements, too. Eva's strengths and secret recipes for enjoying life gave the volunteer encouragement to go on and direct herself toward additional goals. That way, the loss of her primary role as a mother could be replaced by other goals and motivations as she passes through new stages in her life, while never forgetting or making light of previous accomplishments.

These stories illustrate that probably all people can perform their obligation to *bikur cholim,* to the extent that they are capable. The performance of *bikur cholim* can help one fulfill a *mitzvah,* a commandment. In addition to accomplishing this sacred obligation, performing *bikur cholim* frequently can, even if for a fleeting moment, bring inner warmth to the soul, a true sense of being a partner with God in doing good in this world.

# CHAPTER TWO

# *BIKUR CHOLIM* IN JEWISH THOUGHT AND HISTORY

Visiting the sick is widely regarded, both inside and outside the Jewish community, as a good deed. People who spend time with a lonely person confined to a hospital bed or who speak to a grieved person in a time of sadness are regarded as decent and kind.

This is certainly true, but simply being good is not quite the full meaning of a *mitzvah*. A *mitzvah* is a religious obligation. We are required to do it, independent of our feelings. Visiting the sick, *bikur cholim*, is an example of a *mitzvah*.

The *mitzvah* of *bikur cholim* emerges because we are trying to act in God's ways. We are, according to the Torah (the first five books of the Hebrew bible), made in God's image and we are supposed to act accordingly. Therefore, we search out the Torah, Talmud, other sacred writings, Jewish history, our sages, and our own experiences to determine how to act in a Godly manner.

We can determine such acts in several crucial ways. We can look to see the sorts of acts God performed or the acts God willed the Jewish people to do.

At the end of the seventeenth chapter of Genesis, Abraham took Ishmael, his son, and all the males in his household and performed a circumcision. (Abraham was then ninety-nine years old.) Right afterward, as Abraham and the others were recovering, the eighteenth chapter begins with a visit by God to Abraham: "The Lord appeared to him by the terebinths of Mamre . . . " (Genesis 18:1). The Rabbis who wrote the Babylonian Talmud interpreted this event to mean that all people had an obligation to emulate God and visit the sick. "Just as God visited the sick, so, too, you should visit the sick" (*Sotah* 14a).

It is interesting to note parenthetically that the *Shabbat* of Parshat Vayera commemorates this event by re-telling the story and, traditionally, is the day that honors all those who participate in the *mitzvah* of *bikur cholim*.

In addition to emulating God's ways, *bikur cholim* is seen as an act of *gemilut chasadim*, loving-kindness. One daily morning prayer (based on *Mishnah, Peah* 1) includes this statement: "These are the things of which a person enjoys the fruits in this world, while the principal remains in the hereafter, namely: honoring father and mother, practice of kindness, hospitality to strangers, visiting the sick, giving a dowry to the bride, attending the dead to the grave . . . "

*Bikur cholim* is also an example of *tikkun olam* ("repairing the world," or making it holy) and making ourselves *shutafei ha-Kodosh Barukh Hu* (partners with God).

The Talmud is replete with references to *bikur cholim*. For example, in *Nedarim* 39b, Rabbi Akiva went to see one of his disciples who had become sick. No one else would visit the poor man. Akiva walked into the house and "swept and sprinkled the ground before him." After the man had recovered from his illness, he gave thanks to Rabbi Akiva, saying it was the visit that had made him well. Rabbi Akiva went to his other disciples and said, "One who does not visit the sick is like a shedder of blood." In this same chapter and elsewhere, it is stressed that those who perform the *mitzvah* of *bikur cholim* are truly blessed because they take away "a sixtieth part of the sickness." In addition, the Rabbis believed that *bikur cholim* was one of the *mitzvot* for which "a person enjoys the fruits in this world while the principal remains in the world to come" (*Shabbat* 31a).

In *Nedarim* 40a is the statement "One who visits the sick causes them to live." Jews are also enjoined to visit Gentiles "in the interests of peace" (*Gittin* 61a).

Another talmudic story (*Berachot* 5b) involves Rabbi Yochanan. The Rabbi was speaking with Rabbi Elazar, who was a very ill friend. Rabbi Yochanan said, "Give me your hand." Rabbi Elazar did so and soon got up. It is clear from this passage that the Rabbis believed that visiting the sick had curative powers.

Interestingly, Rabbi Yochanan became ill and Rabbi Chanina came to visit. Rabbi Yochanan gave him his hand and rose up well. Later, Rabbi Yochanan visited Rabbi Chanina who himself was now ill. Rabbi Yochanan said that Rabbi Chanina should say the same words of comfort he had once uttered to Rabbi Yochanan. Rabbi Chanina said, "When I was free of sufferings, I could help others; but now that I am myself a sufferer, I must ask others to help me" (*Shir Hashirim Rabba* 11:16).

Beyond telling stories about visiting the sick, the Rabbis offered much practical advice as well.

For example, those who visit the sick are told to be considerate of the ill. Visitors are enjoined not to visit very early in the morning or very late at night (*Nedarim* 40a).

It is important to note that visiting the sick included the idea of helping the person and making sure his or her needs were being met. For instance, Rabbi Eliezer said, "When you visit a sick man who is without means, be quick to offer refreshments to him and he will esteem it as though you did uphold and restore his soul." The sick person should not be left to suffer alone (*Berachot* 5b). According to *Shabbat* 12a, visiting the sick is permitted even on the Sabbath. Indeed, during the Middle Ages it became a custom to visit the sick right after the Sabbath morning services.

*Bikur cholim* is embedded in Jewish law. For example, Maimonides said it was a *mitzvah* to visit the sick (*Hilchot Aveil* as cited in *Yoreh De'ah*, 335:1). The 335th chapter in the *Shulchan Aruch* (*Yoreh De'ah*) is devoted to this subject. The language of the chapter is quite clear: "It is a religious duty to visit the sick."

The importance of the *mitzvah* of *bikur cholim* can be seen in other Jewish writings as well. For example, in his will Rabbi Eleazar the Great wrote: "My son, pay careful attention to visiting the sick, because one who visits him lessens his illness. Entreat him to return to his Creator, and pray for him, and then leave. Let not your presence be a burden to him, because he has enough of a burden with his illness. When you go to visit a person who is sick, enter joyfully, because his eyes and heart are directed to those who enter to visit him."

The twelfth-century book *Sefer Hasidim* (361) said: "If a poor man is sick and a rich man is sick, and people go to visit the rich man in order to show him respect, go you to the poor man, even if the rich man is learned, because there are many people present with him, and no one goes to visit the poor."

The Jewish community has, throughout its history, seen the communal responsibility to take care of the ill. Records of official associations specifically aimed at helping the ill (as opposed to, for example, the community officially hiring physicians and engaging in other efforts) go back to fourteenth-century Spain. In 1336, in Saragossa, a shoemaker's guild made arrangements for caring for the ill. A *bikur cholim* society began in Perpignan in 1380. Similar such societies blossomed in the fifteenth century.

Spanish Jews exiled in 1492 traveled through Europe. The Spanish Jews introduced *bikur cholim* societies to Italy. The idea was so popular that it spread to such places as Prague and then to Central and Eastern Europe.

By the eighteenth century, societies to help the sick were widespread in Germany. One characteristic aspect of such efforts was that individual associations and guilds cared for their members, but *bikur cholim* societies were developed especially to care for the poor who could not take care of themselves.

Legislation about Jews who lived in Galicia at the end of the eighteenth century and in Russia during the first half of the nineteenth century addressed this issue. Societies to help the ill were given legal status, and their regulations were published.

Such societies engaged in a variety of activities. For example, they provided funds for needy travelers, they made sure all Jewish male babies could receive a circumcision (which was considered vital because it was a sign of the Jewish people's covenant with God), they provided medical care for women during childbirth, and much else.

In the eighteenth century, there were women's associations, frequently called *nashim zadkaniyyot* ("pious women"). The members of these associations acted as nurses, visiting women who were ill, preparing the female dead, and performing other related activities.

Sadly, the sense of *bikur cholim* as a *mitzvah* has become somewhat neglected. However, the obligation to do it, the reasons for it, and the central principles for performing it were all present in Jewish sacred literature and in Jewish history.

It is time for *bikur cholim* to be reclaimed as a valuable part of the Jewish heritage.

# CHAPTER THREE

## ILLNESS, DEATH, AND DYING

Every time the volunteer went to visit ninety-nine-year-old Herman, he would greet her with a great big smile. Then, almost immediately, he would start out with a complaint that he wished God would take him and that he would die peacefully in his sleep with no pain.

The volunteer wondered why Herman constantly lamented his life. His health complaints were minor; some of them were the same complaints the fifty-five-year-old volunteer herself was experiencing. These included the beginnings of a cataract in her left eye and pains in her knees on damp days.

Herman was lucid and seldom repeated himself the way some people his age might be expected to do. He frequently went to the nursing home library and read many history books, which he said he did because he recognized the importance of learning and studying as an important part of life.

The volunteer questioned him about his life and listened with interest and understanding as he told his life story. He taught her history firsthand, as a person who had actually been there. She listened carefully to his lament that he could no longer do many of the activities of his younger years. He used to swim a lot and taught his young girlfriends how to swim. Here at the nursing home he has no access to a pool. He can no longer partake of the joys of mountain climbing, an activity that he did until well into his sixties. Mostly, he is in a wheelchair now, but he sometimes takes walks, using his walker for support and mainly for confidence. He can walk without the walker but has fresh memories of recent falls that injured his hips.

The volunteer understands more and more about his request to die, as she meets with him from week to week. He is not suicidal. He is dealing with the fact that life is a process that goes through stages, from the trauma of birth to the peace of death. He is in the last stage, preparing for death.

In order to understand and then perform the *mitzvah* of *bikur cholim*, it is vital to understand the underlying psychological aspects of illness and death that so profoundly affect those in need of being visited. Such an understanding requires an analysis of the various stages of our lives, which culminate in a final stage.

According to psychiatrists and psychologists such as Sigmund Freud and Erik Erikson, humans mature as we pass through certain specific stages in our lives. If we are able to negotiate each stage successfully, we experience a particular sort of growth associated with that stage. After success at one stage, we advance to a new, more complicated stage. This ultimately prepares us for death, which is the final stage of life.

Erikson, a developmental psychologist, builds on Freud's stages of development but suggests concrete stages in which the person has eight specific tasks to negotiate in a designated order. He calls these the eight ages of man, and each stage has special issues or conflicts to deal with. The task required is to deal successfully with each of these conflicts. For example, the first conflict (1) consists of Basic Trust versus Basic Mistrust. The infant learns how to trust that the caretaker who has been there to feed him or her since birth will continue to be there to meet his or her basic needs. Other stages to negotiate include: (2) Autonomy versus Shame and Doubt—which, if negotiated properly, can lead to self-control without the loss of self-esteem, cooperation and willfulness, and freedom of self-expression. Problems in this stage can lead to loss of self-control, suppression of self-expression, and loss of self-esteem. (3) Initiative versus Guilt, which if properly negotiated leads to undertaking, planning, and attacking a task with enthusiasm and an abundance of energy. Problems could be developing a sense of guilt over goals that get out of control and can't be completed. A child might, for example, fantasize himself as being a powerful giant, but in reality he cannot achieve that goal. (4) Industry versus Inferiority: Industry involves doing things with others to accomplish common aims and goals. If people feel they have inadequate skills or tools, they may feel inadequate and inferior. (5) Identity versus Confusion, which usually occurs in youth. The youth begins to understand who he or she is and what his or her interests and potential careers are. (6) Intimacy versus Isolation: Intimacy involves the capacity to commit oneself to specific affiliations and partnerships and to develop ethical strength to abide by these commitments even if they involve sacrifices. Dangers could be isolation or the destruction of others who seem to encroach on one's territory. (7) Generativity versus Stagnation: Generativity involves establishing and guiding the next generation. It can also mean productivity and creativity. (8) Ego Integrity versus Despair is the final stage.

Erikson explains in his book *Childhood and Society* that when people successfully negotiate the tasks through Stage 8, they become post-narcissistic and begin to accept one and only one life cycle as something that has to be, with no substitutions. It becomes the "patrimony of his soul, the seal of his moral paternity of himself. In such final consolidation death loses its sting." In contrast, one who lacks ego integrity fears death and feels despair. Such a person may see life as being too short for any attempt to start over and try alternate roads to find ego integrity.

In the case of Herman, he has prepared himself to reach this final stage because he wishes for it to come to him in a peaceful way. It is not frightening to him, but it is filled with the mystery of the unknown—when, how, and what it will be like to be dead.

There are no definite descriptions in Judaism about life after death. There is no mention in the Jewish bible about a soul being immortal or about a world to come. Traditional Jews believe in the physical resurrection of the body when the Messiah comes. Therefore, autopsies and transplants would be forbidden by someone who believes this way. The late Rabbi Isaac Klein, a Conservative rabbi and the author of *A Guide to Jewish Religious Practice*, states that routine autopsies are forbidden, but autopsies are permitted if doing one could be helpful in curing others or if the law requires it in order to determine cause of death. Also, organ donation would be permitted because there is no greater *kevod hamet* (respect for the dead) than to bring healing to the living, and the body part that is donated will ultimately be buried with the recipient.

According to Rabbi James Rudin, national director of Interreligious Affairs of the American Jewish Committee, more liberal Jews tend to believe that the human spirit transcends death and all souls will dwell with God, and finding God in life is reward enough.

People who become ill before being able to negotiate all the normal stages of life often have more intense issues to deal with. The illness, whether it takes one's life or scares one into understanding the vulnerability of life, illustrates the loss of control over certain parts of our lives. It gives the patient the challenge, after getting over the initial shock, of making choices in handling the situation.

The book *Why Me? Why Anyone?* by Rabbi Hirshel Jaffe, Rabbi James Rudin, and Marcia Rudin illustrates a true-life experience in which Rabbi Jaffe, while in his mid-forties, contracts a mysterious illness called hairy cell leukemia, for which, at that time, there is only experimental treatment. He goes through various mental stages, attempting to handle his feelings as the symptoms of his illness progress from loss of energy to near-death experiences. His good friends, the Rudins, write about their frustrations as they attempt to visit and comfort their dear friend during these visits, through regular phone calls, and by providing child care for his two daughters. They were unsure of what to say at times, but their being there and showing concern was effective.

Elisabeth Kubler-Ross, a renowned psychiatrist and authority on death, proposes that a person dealing with a serious illness negotiates five stages that, in the end, help him or her accept the seriousness of the illness and allow acceptance of impending death. Rabbi Jaffe illustrates, through letters and incidents, the stages he negotiated as he finally began to accept his potential impending death and then, subsequently, his mission when he lived through the crisis—to help others with his disease and with other potentially life-threatening illnesses to find comfort.

Here are the five stages that help a dying person accept impending death after he or she deals with these issues:

Stage One: *Denial and Isolation*—One phrase that is representative of this stage is "it can't be, not me." It is a time of shock and a time to understand that we are mortal and cannot live forever. It is a period of loneliness and isolation from family and friends because they symbolize the outside world, of which the sick person is no longer a member.

Stage Two: *Anger*—Why did it happen to me? What did I do to deserve this? Why, when I give to charity, attend weekly *Shabbat* services, have good relationships with my children, does this happen to me? Why doesn't it happen to the old lady next door instead? She is so mean to people. She always yells at them. Why did God punish me with this?

Stage Three: *Bargaining*—This stage involves an effort to bargain with God. Sufferers typically plead to God, offering to change their religious and ethical behavior and in return asking God to take away the illness. People might, for example, say to God, "I'll increase my donation to charity. I'll be nicer to my children, if only I can live."

Stage Four: *Depression*—The anger from previous stages gets replaced. Now there is a sense of great loss. The patient feels a sense of hopelessness. There are two kinds of depression. One is reactive to the situation: "I'm sick and I'm not go-

21

ing to get better, so what's the use?" The second type has to do with preparing for grief. This type of depression involves an understanding of the situation and a sadness that the losses exist, and it allows the patient to get to the final stage of grief, which creates a sense of relief.

Stage Five: *Acceptance*—If a patient negotiates this stage while alive, it allows him or her to peacefully accept impending death. Such a patient is usually void of feeling angry or depressed. Herman, the ninety-nine-year-old man mentioned at the beginning of this chapter, was ready to die peacefully, and he often expressed that to his volunteer. Close to the time of death, a patient will be losing strength and will want and need fewer visitors than in the past when he or she needed support and reassurance.

There is no set time frame for each stage, and there may not be a fluid passage from one stage to another. A person could go back and forth from one stage to another. One could die before even getting through Stage One. In Elisabeth Kubler-Ross's book *Death, the Final Stage of Life*, she talks about death as being "the key to the door of life." By accepting that each of us has a finite existence, we can then find strength and courage to devote every day of our lives to growing as fully as possible. Denial of death is partially responsible for people living purposeless, wasted lives.

There are certain kinds of illnesses in which it may be more difficult for the patient to negotiate the steps toward an acceptance of death. This may happen because of certain prejudices that society has against a person's lifestyle, such as against someone who is dying of AIDS.

Because high-risk behaviors that are responsible for transmission of the AIDS virus are often socially unacceptable (for example, sharing drug injection equipment or being sexually active with a homosexual, with someone who uses drugs, or with someone who has had multiple sex partners), a patient who has contracted the AIDS virus may feel rejected by society, may have a great deal of self-anger for having chosen a lifestyle that caused the disease, and may as a result need to deny the true illness and hide it from friends and family because it is too painful to be an outcast of society.

Thirty-eight-year-old Joseph S. was a drug addict who had contracted the AIDS virus when he shared needles with a friend. He was in the hospital with pneumonia; he appeared frail and had sunken cheeks. Because of his disease, he was put in a special unit in the hospital. The nurses came in to check his vital statistics but rarely stayed long enough to talk to him. Family and friends called him on the phone but rarely came to visit in person. When they did visit, they stood at a distance from him and only stayed a brief time. They kissed other family members who came to visit, but they never shook his hand or kissed him. He spent most of his day in poor spirits. At first, he denied the seriousness of his pneumonia: "It's just a bad cold, and soon these antibiotics will work, and I'll be able to leave." But the pneumonia worsened, and he needed the help of a respirator to breathe. He lost a lot of weight because he found himself unable to eat. His self-esteem became lower and lower as he berated himself for being the black sheep in his family. No one else used heroin. How could he be so stupid as to get hooked? It was so selfish of him to lead such a lifestyle for just the brief moment of feeling the rush as he shot heroin. He truly hurt his mother when he stole her beautiful ring so he could sell it to buy that momentary bit of pleasure. The thought crossed his mind that if he were given a chance to recover, he would leave the hospital and go right to a local methadone program and would make it work so that he would never have to return to heroin use and its ensuing lifestyle. His family never appeared comfortable visiting. They never brought up the topic of his having AIDS, and he had hurt them enough, so he never said anything. His condition worsened, and he died without resolving many issues with family. They never spoke about the true nature of his disease.

Young children, infants, and toddlers usually have limited understanding about what is happening in their lives. They experience unexplained traumas and pain. They may experience a separation from their parents and/or other family members. Infants who have begun to bond with their parents may now have trouble successfully negotiating Erikson's first stage of development—basic trust versus basic mistrust—if they are removed from the home and their parents are nowhere to be found. Visitors who come on a regular basis could help by easing some pain and giving comfort when the infants' parents can't be there. Two-year-old David was seen by a volunteer three times a week. When the volunteer first met David, she felt uncomfortable, seeing him lying in his crib, and hooked up to many tubes. She was unsure what she could do to help ease his suffering, so she tried to talk to him in a soft voice and stroked his head gently. He was quiet and just lay there, staring at the ceiling. The volunteer was not sure that her visit had really done anything to help David. After thinking about her own teenagers and their good health, she knew she had to return to see David again. She remembered the importance of being available to her children if they woke up sick at night and called to her. They were always more at ease if they were not alone. It took the volunteer a month before she felt that David recognized her as someone familiar to him. She read to him, sang songs, put on puppet shows, and he began to look at her and not stare at the ceiling. Her ritual, when she was about to leave, was to throw him a kiss. She felt a sense of warmth inside when one day, after four months of visiting, he threw her a kiss back. It felt good to see a response from David that showed she had made a difference to him. But she got something else from the visits, too, which she realized was more important than just performing a *mitzvah*. The visits helped her appreciate her teenagers more and improved her relationship with them. Before her *bikur cholim* experiences with David, she had considered her children rebellious and had reacted in anger as they asked for later curfews and more freedom to go places on their own. Now, because she had a new respect for life and appreciated the relative good health of her children, she found herself able to appreciate them more. She was able to sit down and take the time to talk to them and try to understand them better.

Children who are young (four to six years old) but who can verbalize still may have confusion about understanding their illness. Many of them feel helplessness and loss of control. Their siblings and peers are healthy and live at home with their parents. The pain comes and goes for them, and it is both physical and mental. The handicap of illness makes them different from normal children. They feel abandoned by their parents and family since they are the ones who were sent away from home. They blame themselves. It must have been something they did, although they are not sure what, that caused their pain and banishment, to live among strangers. They might not eagerly welcome a *bikur cholim* visitor because they see that person as yet an additional stranger in their series of treatments—someone here for now but gone tomorrow, maybe never or rarely to return. Since parents are having trouble dealing with their child's illness, they often don't say much to help the child understand that he or she is not to blame for the illness. Parents usually don't want to talk much about the prognosis of the illness, as a way of protecting their child from mental pain. The child has had limited life experience and is not sophisticated or knowledgeable enough to understand severe illness or death.

Six-year-old Rebecca had been in and out of the hospital, as her leukemia flared up and then went into remission. She had a nine-year-old brother and a two-year-old sister, both in good health. When the *bikur cholim* volunteer first met her in the hospital, Rebecca was polite but sullen. She answered questions but showed no feelings as she gave her answers, and she asked the volunteer some questions about herself. She wanted to know if the volunteer had children and if her children were nice and behaved well. She also asked about her children's health. The volunteer told her about her fifteen-year-old son and thirteen-year-old daughter and said that their health was good. Rebecca commented that, therefore, they must be good children, but she refused to expand any further when the volunteer asked her why she thought that. The rest of the visit involved the volunteer's asking Rebecca about her likes and dislikes and activities she enjoyed doing. When the volunteer asked if she could come back to visit in two days, Rebecca stated with little emotion in her voice that she guessed it would be okay. The volunteer visited Rebecca for several months, two to three times per week. The volunteer engaged in a lot of play activities with Rebecca, and it seemed to be mainly through play that Rebecca expressed some of her issues of not feeling normal, of being abandoned by family, and of becoming sick because she is bad. The volunteer got to meet Rebecca's parents and was able to provide other volunteers from her synagogue who could help them with things such as child care for the two-year-old so that the mother could visit Rebecca more frequently, with grocery shopping and meal preparation to free up the mother's time, and with some special activities for the nine-year-old so that it would lessen the jealousy he had toward Rebecca for being the center of attention. Whenever his parents visit her, they are away from him, and even when they are with him, they clearly are focusing their attention on his sister's situation and not on him.

Pre-adolescents and teens are more aware of their situation and diagnosis and may want to talk about their fears and ask questions. It may be hard for them to talk about these issues with their parents, who still find it emotionally difficult to deal with the situation and who wish to shelter their children to the extent that it is possible. Volunteers can listen and can also direct the patient to the proper person to answer some of the medical questions.

Fifteen-year-old Jason had been hospitalized due to seizures, which came on suddenly three months ago while at a school dance. Whenever his parents visited, he would ask them questions about the seriousness of his condition and the probability that it would happen again. They assured him that because he was in a teaching hospital and was hooked up to a monitor where they measure seizures, they would find him the right medication, and he would not have to worry. Somehow, he felt they answered too quickly. He really wanted to talk about his feelings and the trauma of the recent incident, but they assured him he'd be fine and steered away from the topic of seizures. A volunteer came to visit him weekly for the month he was hospitalized. Jason spoke to his volunteer about the trauma of the sudden seizures. He talked of being embarrassed because the incident happened in front of his date, whom he had just asked out for the first time, and in front of his friends. The volunteer listened empathetically as Jason poured out his feelings and fears. She was unable to give him any advice or assurance that it would never happen again, but she did ask if she could tell the nurse about his concerns. That way, perhaps the nurse could give him an idea of his condition and what the hospitalization was supposed to do. He thanked her for this and said he felt it would be helpful for him to be informed so that he could have some idea what he would have to deal with. The volunteer came twice after this particular incident, and both times Jason reiterated some of his concerns and fears. He had received helpful information from the nurse and from his doctor. His parents were still not able to listen without changing the subject, but friends were calling and visiting to express their concern, and he could see that they would still be his friends. The doctor and nurses had given him hope that once the right medication and dosage could be prescribed—and that might take time—he could probably lead a normal life. Jason was thankful to the volunteer for being there to listen and to direct him. The volunteer felt good about that, but it was more than just feeling good after performing a *mitzvah*. She learned the importance of listening and not tuning someone out, even if she had no answer to the problems he was expressing. She had a teenage daughter and now began to take time to listen to her daughter. In the past, she realized that she had been too quick to tell her daughter about behavior she did not like and to criticize her. She had never before made any effort to hear what her daughter was thinking or feeling. Jason taught her the importance of listening.

People receiving chemotherapy often must deal with many issues and fears. They may be in a very weakened condition and may have many concerns that they are afraid to ask about. If they do ask, whatever information is given may not be specific enough, and that may be scary. In the past, chemotherapy was associated

27

with the treatment of inoperable cancer. There was often an unspoken assumption that it was a last chance at life, and if it didn't work, death would surely ensue shortly.

Family members of a person receiving chemotherapy may be overwhelmed by the shock of a new diagnosis or by the recurrence of a disease they had hoped was in remission, and they may spend less time with the patient as a result.

One volunteer visited a cancer patient, Diane M., prior to her surgery. Diane was optimistic because her breast lump was discovered early and she felt that the surgery would remove all of the cancer. After the surgery, the volunteer was surprised that Diane was in good spirits in spite of her obvious exhaustion. She made brief visits several times during the first week after the surgery. But then there seemed to be a sudden change in Diane's personality. She became angry and weepy. Her sister, who had visited daily prior to the surgery, came only once that week and only stayed about an hour. Diane mentioned to the volunteer that she needed chemotherapy but gave few details about when. It was obvious to the volunteer that she did not want to deal with it. The volunteer felt awkward. She didn't know what to say, but she sensed that it was important for her to be there for Diane. Sometimes she just sat there and silently held Diane's hand. The volunteer knew Diane appreciated her presence when she felt Diane, after a long period of silence, squeeze her hand. The visits with Diane helped the volunteer understand that she did not have to have all the solutions to life's problems, but that being supportive to others is a big help.

People with Alzheimer's disease and other dementias develop problems in orientation, language, memory, the recognition of family and friends, the recognition of formerly familiar settings, and the performance of everyday tasks. The disease may start out gradually, and family members may take care of the patients. It may, however, progress to a point where the person can no longer think, speak, move, or recognize anyone or anything. It becomes difficult for family members to deal with this deterioration. Adult children whose parents suffer from Alzheimer's disease have difficulty reversing roles, and parents with the beginning stages of Alzheimer's often express guilt for not being able to function as they had before.

One volunteer was introduced to Robert G. in the Alzheimer's unit of the nursing home where he volunteered. He spent a half-hour with Robert and felt frustrated because every few minutes Robert would ask him his name and whether he was married and had any children. The volunteer patiently answered the questions but after about fifteen minutes felt frustration that his answers were meaningless because the same questions kept being repeated. He noticed Robert's daughter's frustrations. As she was leaving, the volunteer overheard her say to her father: "Dad, it's all right to wear a diaper. Everyone here does." The volunteer wondered whether he should continue to visit. Did Robert benefit from having visitors if he could not remember who they were or whether they had even been there to see him. He decided to visit a few more times before judging the value of the visit, and he was glad he did. Robert did not ever know him by name but nearly always seemed happy to have a visitor. The big smile that flashed across Robert's face as the volunteer patted him on the shoulder or put his arm around him made the volunteer see the importance of touch and of being there. As a result, he began to understand the value of human contact to all people. At home, he began to put his arms around his son and to talk to him more about his job and his volunteer work, and their relationship grew closer, too.

Some additional situations of illnesses concern the problems of stroke victims, amputees, and paralyzed victims. These people are suffering traumas through the loss of either physical parts of the body or the loss of normal body functioning. They go through the grief stages as delineated by Elisabeth Kubler-Ross.

One volunteer visited Ellen T., who recently had a leg amputated due to diabetes. When the volunteer first met Ellen, Ellen was berating herself for not taking care of her diabetes and was very depressed. Ellen spoke about how she would now be a slave to a wheelchair and how she could not deal with being dependent on family members to get around. Now she was a burden. The volunteer knew it was wrong to give false reassurance to Ellen, so she just listened and allowed the patient to vent her anger and frustrations. She visited Ellen for many months and noted her progress as Ellen started to accept her loss and began physical therapy to allow herself more independence. Ellen was generally more happy and spoke to the volunteer about her hope that in the upcoming future, after her stump healed, she could be fitted for a prosthesis. At times, Ellen would revert back to her weepiness and depression, and the volunteer felt okay about being there just to hold her hand. Ellen thanked her for being there, but the volunteer really meant it when she told Ellen that she should be the one to thank her. Through her visits to Ellen, the volunteer learned to appreciate life and be thankful for her family's good health. Even though the family had had some financial problems recently, she could now see that they still had what was most important in life—good health.

The following are some general rules that seem to help patients cope with their illnesses: (1) A patient who is informed about the illness and the prognosis is usually better able to cope. Uncertainty opens up a gateway for the imagination, for anxiety due to uncertainty. (2) Questions should be answered, if the patient asks. Whatever positive aspects exist should be discussed so that the patient is not made to feel there is no hope. Positive aspects could even be expressed in terms of small possible steps of improvement, even if they may only be short term. (3) If patients are in denial about the seriousness of the situation, facts should not be thrust upon them. The denial may be a way of coping that patients need for the moment. (4) Patients fare better if they feel support, which may be in the form of a person being there to listen and to hold their hand. Ultimately, patients will come to terms with the situation in the way they are able to. (5) A false rosy picture painted by the family too often prevents the patient from expressing feelings and final issues to family members for fear of hurting them.

The purpose of this chapter has been to provide an understanding of patients and the traumas they experience as they learn of their illness and begin to let its meaning sink in fully, the stages they go through in dealing with the prognosis and progression, and the inner peace they can achieve as they learn acceptance and understand death and trauma as a normal part of life. In order to become an effective *bikur cholim* volunteer, one should understand how and why the patient might relate to a visit at a particular phase and how to help the patient work through these feelings. This chapter also illustrates through examples that in addition to performing a *mitzvah*, the volunteer very often benefits on a personal level.

The next chapter will deal with the person who performs the *mitzvah* of *bikur cholim*. Now that volunteers understand some of the traumas of illness and fragility, they are better able to see ways in which their visits can benefit patients as well as themselves. Chapter 4 will deal with some of the fears that volunteers experience and how they can be overcome.

# CHAPTER FOUR

# COMMON FEARS ABOUT VISITING THE SICK—WHY PEOPLE DON'T VISIT

A lot of people want to visit the sick. They know it is the right thing to do. They are supposed to try to make others feel better. They were taught that to visit the sick is a *mitzvah*. Yet, when the time comes for the actual visit, many people find themselves uneasy or even unable to go. There are a lot of reasons for this.

It is important for those who would like to visit the sick to face their potential fears by understanding both their cause and their cure. It is therefore crucial to examine the psychological impediments that people may face. Some of these impediments are as follows:

**1.** Difficulty Facing Someone Who Is in Failing Health or Dying

What can one say to someone who is frail and may never be able to take part in the usual activities of life? What can one say or do for someone who is dying? What can one do for someone who does not appear to be conscious and cognizant that there is even a visitor present? These are some of the questions that quite understandably go through the mind of a person planning to visit the elderly or the ill. It is crucial to face them prior to performing the *mitzvah* of *bikur cholim*.

Gertrude had an eighty-nine-year-old aunt in a nursing home. She planned to visit her aunt at least once a month. This aunt was her late mother's older sister, who had never married and who had lived at home with her parents for many years, giving them nurturing care in their older years. Gertrude had fond memories of the many family celebrations of Jewish holidays that were frequently held at her grandparents' and aunt's home. When her grandfather hid the *afikomen* during the Passover *seder*, her aunt used to pull Gertrude aside and reveal the hiding place. Each year everyone remarked that Gertrude must have such great detective skills, because without fail, she would be the first to find the *afikomen*.

Her aunt was in good physical health but had Alzheimer's disease. She often repeated the same questions to Gertrude and usually did not even recognize her as her niece. She would talk to Gertrude about her family as if Gertrude were a stranger. Gertrude could not stand to see an aunt whom she always thought about with fond memories, now being so frail and helpless. She sometimes canceled planned visits because she reasoned that it didn't really matter to her aunt if she did not come. After all, the aunt didn't usually know who she was, anyway.

Then one day during Passover, Gertrude came to see her aunt and brought some *matzah*, *haroset*, gefilte fish, and wine, along with a *Haggadah*. Her aunt lived in a nursing home that had only a few Jewish residents, and so there were limited Jewish holiday celebrations. When her aunt saw the *matzah*, the old woman's memories came pouring out, memories of Pesach *seder* celebrations and the mouth-watering foods she had cooked for the family. Even though she still did not recognize Gertrude as family, she said she felt ready to adopt Gertrude as a daughter. She reminisced with joy about her holiday celebrations, and Gertrude learned her family history firsthand. Also, Gertrude came to the realization that she was able to provide for her aunt a re-entrance, in at least a small way, into the Jewish community from which the woman had been torn away when she entered the world of this particular nursing home. This realization helped give meaning to the *bikur cholim* Gertrude was nearly ready to give up. Almost every Friday before *Shabbat*, Gertrude came to see her aunt and brought along some of the traditional *Shabbat* foods—chicken, chicken soup, potato kugel, gefilte fish, challah, and wine for *Kiddush*. Gertrude began to gain a deeper meaning of the culture of Judaism. It was more than just a religion; it was a way of life. She also learned that there were two more Jewish residents at this particular home, and she made an effort to visit them briefly at least once a month and to return their culture to them by sharing food and hearing their stories.

Thus, Gertrude's difficulty in dealing with her aunt's frailty was overcome as she found herself able to understand that life changes as we grow older. The memories she carried of her aunt were her childhood memories. Just as Gertrude had grown up and was no longer that little girl who felt the excitement of spending a holiday meal with her family and grandparents, so, too, had her aunt grown older and more frail, as her grandparents had been. Gertrude also now fully understood that the customs and culture we grow up with become ingrained in us. Her mission as a visitor to her elderly aunt and to the other Jewish residents became to give them back the Judaism that had been snatched away when they moved from their homes and familiar surroundings. Their memories, which they shared with her, enriched her sense of Judaism.

Understanding the stages of life and the realities of illness and death is a prerequisite to being an effective visitor. Of course, reading and talking with others is a good place to begin.

It also helps to role-play. Have someone pretend to be the ill person and try to express your feelings. Visualize such visits as well.

### 2. Personal Fears of Illness or Death

Many times parents shield their children from visiting sick and dying people on the grounds that it is something a child should not have to deal with. Some parents truly believe they are protecting their children and feel that confronting death will traumatize or harm children in a certain way. One useful approach here is to discuss the situation with the child.

More crucial for this book, however, is the possibility that parents themselves do not know how to deal with illness and death. Being involved with the ill and dying brings thoughts of one's own mortality. Thoughts such as the following might be stirred up: "I could be the one who's dying, but I'm not ready to die. I still have my children to take care of. I haven't even had a chance for a career, and so forth. I know I should visit, but if I don't see the person, I won't have to think about death now. If I did visit, what would I say? How could I possibly comfort someone when I feel so sad and might start crying while I'm there? I have to be strong if I'm going to visit, and I just can't be. I'll just make the patient more upset."

I remember, as a ten-year-old child, hearing my mother say that she had to go to a funeral because one of her good friends had died suddenly of a cerebral hemorrhage. I had known this friend, who had lived in our old neighborhood. My mother was noticeably upset but would not say anything more. Any questions I asked, she just assured me that this was nothing for me to worry about. I spent several years after that wondering about death. I really understood no more about death except that it was mysterious and that the person disappeared and was placed in a box in the ground. Many questions about death haunted me. Was it scary to be dying? Did a dying person suffer a lot of pain? Can a child die? Is it a lonely process? Do people abandon someone who is dying? I couldn't ask anyone these questions. My parents said I didn't have to deal with such questions since I was only a child.

When my mother-in-law was dying from cancer thirty years after that incident, I knew I couldn't do to my children what had been done to me. My mother-in-law was from the same generation as my parents. She said we should not bring the grandchildren to see her. She didn't want them to suffer from seeing her in failing health. She didn't want them to remember her that way.

Yet I knew that since she had lived for her children and grand-children, it would be cruel to have her spend her dying days abandoned by them. Why should a dying person be punished for dying? Besides, there have been many cultures where several generations live together, and just as birth is a family event, so, too, is death just naturally understood to be a part of life's normal cycle.

We brought our four children—then ages seven, nine, eleven, and fourteen—to visit briefly with their grandmother. Their visits seemed to give her extra strength as she reached out her arms to embrace them. She remained at home for most of her dying months, in a familiar setting with home health aides and family. She did not want friends and acquaintances to visit as she prepared to die. She welcomed the support of family visits. She felt comfortable as she went through her possessions and told her sons what she wanted them to have. When taken to the hospital, away from the familiar settings, she died within twenty-four hours.

Eight years later our children still have fond memories of their relationship with their grandmother. They do not dwell on the period when she was dying but talk rather about a variety of memories of gatherings and activities with their grandmother throughout their lives. My youngest daughter has given away many childhood toys that she has outgrown, but she has a small memory box in which she keeps treasures, such as the last doll her grandmother gave her. She also still wears the Jewish star necklace that her grandmother gave her, but only on special occasions so that it does not get lost or broken.

Performing *bikur cholim* may actually aid in people's maturing, in the sense of helping them to become better able to deal with mortality and to see life as a continuum while assessing their current place in that continuum and how they might plan the rest of their lives. Therefore, it is precisely those people with such concerns who can benefit the most from performing *bikur cholim*.

**3.** Fear That the Person Is Too Ill and Being There Will Mean That the Volunteer Is in the Way

This, to some extent, has to do with part of what was just discussed. What can one say to comfort a dying person since volunteers believe that they have no control over whether a person will get better or die? That is true, but what they do have control over is the quality of that person's life during the dying period. How can a volunteer give false hope and say everything will be okay when it might not be? Yet it might also be very uncomfortable for the volunteer to acknowledge to the patient his impending death.

A fifty-five-year-old woman was coming back to visit her critically ill mother after a dinner break. She walked up to the door and heard her mother's voice talking to someone. She decided to wait before entering because, during the other times she had visited, she usually sat silently in front of her mother or talked to her mother to reassure her that she would be okay—although she knew within herself that her mother was truly dying. Her mother rarely replied to her idle chatter.

When after a half-hour the volunteer left the room, she introduced herself and asked what the volunteer had done to get her mother to become so verbal. She was very surprised at the volunteer's reply. "Your mother wanted to talk, and she knew I was ready to listen. I just sat next to her and held her hand, and she poured out her life story to me. She is a really sweet lady."

John Bowlby, a psychologist who studied attachment and loss, found that babies who are given adequate food, water, and warmth but deprived of tough and of being held show retarded emotional and physical development. Emotional and physical symptoms also occur in adults who are "undertouched," such as the sick and the aged. In hospital settings even the mildest touch by a nurse or physician reassures and comforts.

What's crucial in dealing with this concern is simply asking the person, the person's family, and medical personnel about the appropriateness of a visit, its length, and even its potential contents. This is a practical concern, but one that has a solution.

**4.** Many People Are Uncomfortable Visiting Patients in the Hospital or Nursing Home Setting

There are many potential solutions to this problem. If you are visiting at a nursing home, take the patient to a main meeting room, which is usually decorated with holiday or seasonal themes, or outside, if weather permits, to see plants and gardens. If the patient is confined to bed, bring pictures or decorations to brighten up the room. Or, still better, get young children involved by having them draw get well cards for patients, and talk to them about the theme of *bikur cholim* and where their cards will go.

**5.** Not Having Enough Time to Do *Bikur Cholim*

Some people claim that "Visiting the sick is a nice thing to do, but I work full time and just can't fit it into my schedule." Usually this is just an excuse to cover up some of the fears discussed earlier, and it also could mean that *bikur cholim* is just not a priority on a person's list of things to do. Instead of admitting to these fears, it is much easier to claim to have no time in one's busy schedule.

My own synagogue, North Shore Jewish Center in Port Jefferson Station, New York, does not have a regular, sustained *bikur cholim* program. Every Christmas Day that does not fall on *Shabbat*, a program is set up in which families can come to a local hospital to distribute flowers and talk to patients in the hospital. The children in the Hebrew school make holiday cards for patients. The turnout of volunteers is over thirty people, and the volunteer time is approximately two hours on a day when most people do not work. There can always be time to do a deed if one truly wants to do it. The key, which is one of the aims of this book, is to help people understand *bikur cholim* not just as a good deed that anyone can do but also as an act that we all need to do in order to enrich and bring more meaning to our lives. And *bikur cholim* can be done at various levels so that one can select a level of comfort.

**6.** *Bikur Cholim* Doesn't Mean Enough

When people tell me that *bikur cholim* is too difficult in relationship to the benefits received, I recall the stories of two special men. To me, they exemplify people who found meaning in their lives by making decisions to take a difficult path, choosing their values over an easier, less risky path. They risked their lives in order to find true meaning. Their stories show that, finally, *bikur cholim* is even more than a *mitzvah*. It is a life-affirming activity so powerful that it can provide a central strand of meaning in a person's life.

Let me tell you about those men.

Leo Baeck was a German rabbi who was an army chaplain during World War I. He remained in Germany during the Holocaust even though he had invitations to serve as a rabbi abroad. His mission was to remain with the last *minyan* of Jews in Germany for as long as possible. In 1943, when he was seventy years old, he was deported to Theresienstadt concentration camp and took an active part in helping his people keep faith. He lived his philosophy to become a "witness of his faith."

Viktor Frankl, a psychiatrist and neurologist from Vienna, was in several concentration camps, such as Auschwitz and Dachau, during World War II. His experiences and work while in these severe conditions helped guide others to stay alive during these times by urging them to look ahead to what they wanted to accomplish in the future. For him, these goals were to be alive to reunite with other family members who might also survive and to rewrite and complete the book that he was in the middle of writing when he was uprooted from his home. Sometimes, by having goals in life, we can survive temporary hardships through knowing that our lives can become more enriched by the hard work it took to achieve our goals.

If we can see Baeck and Frankl using hard work to get past obstacles, perhaps we will have the courage to get over our initial fright about performing *bikur cholim*. By trying it, we can enrich our lives with the experience. When we visit the sick and dying, we can see the things in our own lives for which we can be thankful. We can become more compassionate and show appreciation for our own lives and families. It also helps give us a fuller connection to our culture and to the Jewish community.

Chapter 5 will be about how to pick the *bikur cholim* setting and how to get started in the process. With the courage to work on enriching our lives, we can begin the process at a level that is comfortable for us.

# CHAPTER FIVE

# AFTER THE DECISION: STEPS TO TAKE IN VISITING THE SICK

Comfort and benefit are the most important aspects of taking any action. If an action is too uncomfortable, a person will do all he can to avoid performing it. These avoidance mechanisms include pretending to or actually forgetting that a commitment was made to perform the action, substituting another obligation for it and justifying why that substitute obligation was more important, and being undependable without giving any reason (hoping that if the obligation is ignored, it will just disappear).

If one can see some benefit in taking an action, then one can tolerate some discomfort. That is why it is important to take steps as slowly as necessary in order to minimize the discomfort. I call these careful steps the READY process. They stand for the following step-by-step actions, which will be discussed in more detail in this chapter:

R—Read and research about *bikur cholim*, including personal experience stories as well as justifications for performing it.
E—Explore existing *bikur cholim* programs.

A—Access the specific programs that would seem to benefit you.

D—Have a dialogue with people involved in these programs, such as directors, volunteers, and also patients who receive the services, if possible.

Y—You! This involves searching within yourself now that you have most of the facts. Have I selected a program that I feel I could be comfortable with and that I could grow with, one that would benefit me and that I would be able to commit to participating in?

## READ AND RESEARCH

In this section I will suggest going to libraries and bookstores to obtain books that might help you understand experiences that could result from performing *bikur cholim*. I have selected some books that you might not be aware of that I feel could be very beneficial to read.

I begin with *Man's Search for Meaning* by Viktor Frankl. There are two parts to this book. In the first part Dr. Frankl describes his experiences as a prisoner in several concentration camps during World War II. He illustrates the severe conditions and talks about his ways of coping with these by detaching himself from as much of these conditions as he could and making his own world. Because he knew he had a purpose in surviving, a task he needed to complete, he willed that he would try to survive.

In the second part he discusses living life to its fullest through the principle of logotherapy—finding missions in one's life that one can strive to achieve and thereby find fulfillment and meaning. Logotherapy is based on "three main pillars," as Frankl labels them. These are freedom of will (freedom for man to take a stand on whatever conditions come his way), the will to meaning, and the meaning of life. The striving and hard work of the *bikur cholim* process helps make success more rewarding and meaningful, as one continues to practice it and perfect its skills.

After my own hospitalization in 1990 and my weekly volunteer visits to the sick, beginning approximately one year later, I wrote a letter to Dr. Frankl in Vienna to inquire where there might be a course on logotherapy given on the East Coast. I described my situation and sent him a published article that illustrated how my interpretation of logotherapy had helped me as I performed *bikur cholim*. He indicated that he did not know of a logotherapy course being offered in my area and included some very kind and encouraging words, saying that what I was doing was very important and that I should continue to perform *bikur cholim*.

Another book that I would recommended is *Why Me? Why Anyone?*, by Rabbi Hirschel Jaffe, James Rudin, and Marcia Rudin. This touching and easy-to-read book describes the trials that Rabbi Jaffe endures as he is diagnosed with a rare form of leukemia. The book is written through letters and descriptions of feelings as Rabbi Jaffe goes through many stages, from being a healthy marathon runner to a critically ill person dependent on experimental drugs to save his life. Besides being written from the patient's point of view, there are chapters written by two very good friends, Rabbi James Rudin and Marcia Rudin. These chapters illustrate the difficulties the Rudins had in performing the *mitzvah* of *bikur cholim*. There were times when they could not visit their friend because he was too sick or too depressed to have visitors. They described the frustration of not knowing what to say when they did visit and saw how gravely ill their friend was. When they could not perform the *mitzvah* of the visit, they performed *bikur cholim* in other ways, such as taking care of the rabbi's two daughters so that his wife could be with him full-time.

*Why Me? Why Anyone?* shows that even rabbis, who usually have the experience of *bikur cholim*, do not always find it so easy to perform. But the benefits after the struggle far outweigh the struggle.

A third recommendation is *Six Parts Love*, by Roni Rabin. This is a biography written by the author about her father, David, and their whole family from the time her father discovered he had ALS

(Lou Gehrig's disease) through the step-by-step deterioration of his physical condition. With the continued love and support of his wife and their four children, he mentally and medically survived the severe progression of his disease and was able to live at home throughout the ordeal. This book has vivid illustrations portraying how many people who had been good friends shunned David and the rest of the family as the disease progressed. Probably because they were unable to deal with immortality, they were unable to face the potential death of a formerly vibrant friend and colleague. Both David and his wife were doctors, and it was other doctors who, despite routinely dealing with life and death matters, were unable to be there for their colleague. Even David's wife was treated as a widow while David's disease was progressing. People would either try to avoid her or, if they saw her, would rarely inquire about David's health. Once when David had fallen on the ground in the parking lot of the hospital where he worked, a colleague walked right by him and left him lying there. A key message in this book is that *bikur cholim* is important because it shows the patient and his family that people do care. Being there and showing compassion is all that is requested from a patient. David was aware that his ALS was a debilitating disease that would grow progressively worse until death, yet because he had the continued support from his family and a few friends and relatives, he was able to accept the deteriorations as they occurred and live as normal a life as possible. Until his death, he continued work on an endocrinology research grant that he had obtained, kept active with other writing, and encouraged the members of his family to achieve what they were capable of doing. It is a very touching book and clearly illustrates the importance of *bikur cholim*.

A fourth book, called *Give Me Your Hand* by Jane Handler and Kim Hetherington with Rabbi Stuart L. Kelman, is a concise but thorough, easy to read, and practical guide to visiting the sick. It begins by discussing the religious reasons and obligations for *bikur cholim*, then describes how to perform *bikur cholim*, including do's and don'ts. The book also covers various types of illnesses, what kinds of needs different patients have, and how to act to best meet these needs. The conclusion describes the benefit of *bikur cholim* with this command: "Feel enriched and empowered by the *mitzvah* of *bikur cholim* for indeed the benefit flows not only to the person who is ill but to you the visitor; it is as if you were the one who asked the patient 'Give me your hand,' and rose up stronger and straighter because of the touch" (page 50). In an appendix this book has prayers, a checklist of do's and don'ts for visitors, and finally some quotes from well-known rabbis regarding the importance of performing *bikur cholim*.

Another book that may be beneficial, especially to someone who is nervous about not knowing what to say to a patient, is *Finding the Right Words* by Wilfred Bockelman. Chapter 4, titled "What to Say to Someone Who Is Terminally Ill," gives specific situations and how they were or could be handled. It also explains the normal stages one goes through in the death process and how to use this knowledge while practicing *bikur cholim*.

Chapter 6 of Bradley Shavit Artson's book *It's a Mitzvah! Step-By-Step To Jewish Living* is an excellent source to help one understand the reasons to perform *bikur cholim*, reasons why many are resistant to doing it, and how to do it in order to alleviate these tensions and fears and actually gain positive experiences from it.

A book called *A Heart of Wisdom*, edited and introduced by Susan Berrin, addresses the issue of aging. This is important because many of the patients we visit when we perform *bikur cholim* are elderly. In the book she discusses statistics compiled by the North American Jewish Data bank, based on the 1990 Jewish Population Study. Since 1971 there has been a 6 percent increase of Jews in the United States over age sixty-five. Jews sixty-five and older make up 18 percent of the total Jewish population. The anticipated increase in the year 2010 will be 22 percent.

The essays include anecdotal experiences; biblical studies on how to treat the elderly so that as they age, which is a normal cycle of life, they do not feel useless and degraded; and suggestions on how to use the experiences of the elderly to help benefit everyone, with the older person as a teacher of history and life

47

experiences and the younger person as the student. The essays also suggest using ceremonies for all kinds of experiences. For example, Cary Kozberg, director of rabbinical and pastoral services for a nursing home, suggests a special ceremony to consecrate the moment of transition into a nursing home.

Through this book we come to understand again as a normal part of life, learn to accept the limitations of aging, and also learn how to use the experiences of aging to benefit ourselves and others. Each essay shows how the person who takes the time to have a relationship with an aged person can grow.

An excellent children's book, called *Grandma Didn't Wave Back* by Rose Blue, is written from the viewpoint of Debbie, a ten-year-old girl whose grandmother lives with her and her parents at the beginning of the story. Debbie was five and a half when her grandfather died, and she recalled her parents and two older brothers going to his funeral, but she was left with some friends while they went. No one explained anything to her about death or funerals, although she intuitively knew some things and was told other things by a peer whom she had never really liked very much. This peer said: "Oh, you know what happens when people die. They have a funeral and they dig a hole and put them in the ground." And Debbie thought of her grandfather deep in the ground and always in the dark, and it made her sick.

At the opening of the story Debbie is now seeing her grandmother grow old and senile. When her grandmother is not sick, she waves to Debbie from the window of their apartment as Debbie comes home from school. When her grandmother's disease is acting up, she stares out the window and does not wave back to Debbie.

As the story continues, grandma's disease progresses to the point at which Debbie's parents feel a need to put her into a nursing home. They try to shelter Debbie as much as possible, but Debbie is aware of what is happening. She comes home from school one afternoon, and her parents inform her that grandma went to live in a nursing home today. Debbie asks to take the bus alone that afternoon to visit her grandmother and bring some of grandma's possessions to her. Her parents allow her to do so, because they somehow begin to realize that they cannot always shelter her in life from what they perceive to be painful experiences.

Debbie's first feelings when she finds her grandmother sitting alone are how horrible it must be for her grandmother to stay in a place away from her family and everyone who loved her. She had brought Grandma a windup clock that her grandmother had had for many years, and this clock, to Debbie, means Grandma's life. As long as it remains wound, Grandma will live. Grandma wants to give back the clock to Debbie, but instead for now they both agree that Grandma will keep it and that Debbie will come often to visit her grandmother and to wind the clock. As Debbie leaves and walks on the beach outside the nursing home, she sees her grandmother at the window waving to her, a sign that for now things are all right. Debbie's visit has brought her grandmother back to good health for now.

Not only is this book a good way to approach illness with young children, but it also helps parents see that sometimes certain subjects need to be talked about so that young children can express fears and receive comfort and so that even young children can be enriched by participating in *bikur cholim*.

These are just a few of many books available to deal with various aspects of *bikur cholim*. The bibliography lists additional articles and resources.

Another part of research includes checking computer Web sites. All one need do is turn to the World Wide Web, type in *bikur cholim*, and go to a search engine such as Alta Vista (www.altavista.com) or Hot Bot (www.hotbot.com), or Webcrawler (www.webcrawler.com). A wealth of information can be obtained.

For example, Bikur Cholim of Denver describes what it is, how it is funded, and the many services it offers: visitation—home or hospital visits to the patient; support for the patient's family; Kosher food, for out-of-town patients and their families to be close to the hospital; blood donor programs, directed toward a specific patient's needs, and Jewish community blood drives; transportation to medical appointments, to meet a patient or a family member at the airport, for shopping, or as needed; medical liaison to help answer general questions that arise during hospitalizations, to provide an interpreter to communicate with care providers, or to assist patients with insurance issues; and chaplaincy services—meeting with a rabbi of the patient's orientation. Then information is given on who to contact by phone or e-mail.

Another entry is from the Jewish Healing Exchange, which is devoted to serving the public by providing reliable information on the Torah Healing Tradition. It lists several materials that can be accessed, such as: A Call to Live, The Secret of Healing, Psalms and Prayers for Healing, Redemption of the Soul (*Pidyon Nefesh*), Rambam (Maimonides) on the Art of Healing, The Baal Shem Tov as a Healer, and King Hezekiah and the Book of Remedies.

## EXPLORE EXISTING BIKUR CHOLIM PROGRAMS

After you know that you would like to volunteer, the next logical question is usually where do you go to find out what programs are available, and how do you pick the one that is best for you?

The Coordinating Council on Bikur Cholim (130 East 59th Street, New York, NY 10022, Room 517) publishes a "Directory of Bikur Cholim Resources" that includes synagogue programs across the United States and Canada and in seventeen other foreign countries.

Also, check local phone books for synagogues in the area and contact them to find out about any official volunteer programs or specific needs for volunteers, even if the synagogue does not have an established *bikur cholim* program.

Contacting Jewish agencies such as Jewish Family Services, JASA (Jewish Association for Services to the Aged), Jewish community centers, and senior citizens programs may reveal more information on existing *bikur cholim* resources in the area.

Hotlines and volunteer coordinating agencies, which exist in some areas, can also be very helpful. Sometimes mailings that solicit contributions for a specific program may be an excellent resource. For example, a recent mailing from Dorot (with the logo "generations helping generations") explains how their volunteers help the Jewish elderly with services such as friendly visiting, kosher meals for the homebound elderly, and emergency food and shelter to homeless elderly. They reconnect the frail elderly to the community of which they had been a part.

Part of the process of exploring existing programs is to find out what is available, but a most important part is to also discover within yourself what your talents and abilities are and what kind of volunteer tasks you feel capable of performing at this time. Do you feel most comfortable with a telephone visit to a homebound person? Can you deliver meals to the homebound or transport an ill person to a medical appointment? What about visits to people's homes to help reconnect them to the outside world and to their Jewish culture? If the homebound experience is something you feel comfortable trying, the key to success is to get the right match. The important thing at this point is that you explore something you feel comfortable with. If you pick something because it's objectively a good action to take but it terrifies you, then it will be too hard to make the commitment to do it regularly. Choose what is basically comfortable, or just a little uncomfortable but not so much that you cannot experience growth.

Are you comfortable being a Buddy to an AIDS-infected person? Too many people with AIDS are prejudged by society and are labeled in a derogatory way because of the activity that caused them to contract the disease, and/or they are shunned because of misconceptions regarding the possibility of catching the disease.

Are you comfortable volunteering with a hospice patient and/ or the family? Will knowing that the death of this person is imminent be a problem for you? Will seeing someone who is critically ill be something you cannot handle?

These are all problems to explore within yourself before you attempt to see about the match.

If you know a specific program you would like to get involved in, you could call that hospital, that nursing home, or that *bikur cholim* society chairperson and speak to the director of volunteers, thus beginning the next small step of the READY process before making a commitment to volunteer.

## ACCESS PROGRAMS OF INTEREST

This is a narrowing-down process. Now that you know why you want to perform *bikur cholim*, are aware of what *bikur cholim* in general entails, and know more about the kinds of programs that exist in your area, you are ready to explore the specific places to volunteer. You are ready to attempt to find a match.

If you have chosen a hospital setting, obtain a list of hospitals in your area and set up appointments to visit, or ask questions on the phone. Make a list ahead of time of some of the questions you would like to have answered.

A sample list of questions and considerations could be as follows: (1) Where is this hospital, home, or nursing home located? Is it a long drive to get there? (2) Are there certain days or times to volunteer, and is there also a minimum number of hours that one is required to volunteer? (3) What kinds of volunteer assignments are available? Are these tasks something I could feel comfortable about performing? (4) Are there any kinds of training available to make me feel more comfortable with my assignment? (5) What are the patients like? Are they receptive to volunteers? (6) If you have visited the place, assess your feelings about the setting. Go by your gut feelings. Are you comfortable at this place? If you don't feel comfortable, you may not want to continue. You will look for an excuse to avoid coming regularly.

If you are working through a *bikur cholim* society, perhaps they have group visits. If this is your first time volunteering and you are nervous about going alone, you might want to try the process in a group. That way, your direct involvement can be as little or as much as you feel comfortable with. If, for example, the group is running a bingo game at a nursing home, you could call the numbers, transport patients from their rooms, or pick specific residents to help with their cards.

Once you have obtained answers to these and any additional questions you might think of, you need to think about the match. This is the next step of the process—dialogue.

## DIALOGUE

The best way to make a final decision is to view the setting and speak to the people involved. These include the director, employers, other volunteers, and patients who receive your services.

Discuss with the volunteer director the job description and its requirements and the training that is available. Do you feel that you can make a good effort to complete job requirements? Are the tasks ones that you feel comfortable with? Do the tasks use your talents effectively? Do you have suggestions for different or additional tasks that may use some of your talents? If so, speak to the director about these and see if it is okay to try them. The director knows the patients and their needs and might feel that some of what you want to do could create potential problems. For example, you might want to bring some snacks on one of your visits to a patient, and you would need to know beforehand if a particular patient is diabetic and cannot eat a birthday cake that is baked with sugar. It will help in your *bikur cholim* work to know the rules and job description ahead of time and to feel comfortable that if you have any questions or issues while you are volunteering, you will have access to the director to discuss these.

Take a tour of the setting. Are you comfortable with the particular setting? Do you feel that you can perform the job adequately, and with additional training could you grow from performing the *bikur cholim* tasks described by the volunteer director?

Speak to the paid staff. Do they treat you with respect? Do they see the value of having a volunteer?

Observe other volunteers. Do they appear to be comfortable in their jobs? Talk to them about the benefits they receive from volunteering. Ask about the possibility of accompanying another volunteer who can introduce you to patients and staffpersons and who can also fill you in about experiences and growth.

Think about your experience in dialoguing for a few days, and try this at several places if you find more than one setting of interest. Then comes the final step in this READY process, which probably is the most important step—You.

## YOU

Sometimes it is so much easier to do research and explore resources. These are necessary steps to prepare you for *bikur cholim*, but now comes the hardest part of the process. This involves making the commitment, saying, "Yes, I can do it. Yes, I will make the commitment to doing *bikur cholim* at this agency, which I have carefully selected." Often, it also involves feeling scared and wondering how will I do it? What will I say to the patient? Will the person like me? Can my visit benefit the patient?

In my volunteer work at a medical hospital, beginning in 1991, I find that each time I go into a room to meet a patient I still get butterflies in my stomach as I think about whether I am intruding on the person. But then I think back to my hospitalization in 1990, and I have vivid memories of the loneliness I felt. I always ask the patient directly if I can visit, being careful to phrase it in such a way that the patient won't feel an obligation to say "yes" just to be polite, when "no" was really what was meant. Even with patients whom I have known for several weeks, I still use that approach.

Once that commitment is made to try *bikur cholim* at the place you have selected, you are ready to take the next step—how to do it. Chapter 6 will cover developing *bikur cholim* skills.

# CHAPTER SIX

## DEVELOPING *BIKUR CHOLIM* SKILLS

Now that you have found the best potential place to volunteer, the next step in the *bikur cholim* process involves learning the specific skills needed to perform *bikur cholim* well. Learning skills is important for volunteers, not simply to give them the necessary confidence to do the job well, but also to make the whole notion of *bikur cholim* more serious and professional. Training is not difficult or lengthy, but it is certainly valuable.

Most agencies give some basic kind of volunteer training before a person begins the process, but many of the training sessions are very brief and just attempt to orient the volunteer to the place and the needs of the program. Too often, they do not address the actual skills a volunteer needs to feel comfortable with the process. That is why I would like to suggest that potential volunteers carefully read two manuals and one paperback book that are available, to prepare themselves for their missions.

*"Yad L 'Yad": A Training Manual for Bikur Cholim Volunteers* by Nina Dubler Katz, with editors Jonathan Katz and Vickie Rosenstreich, was written as a result of requests from communities across the United States who were looking for guidance in

initiating *bikur cholim* programs. The manual is sponsored by the Coordinating Council on Bikur Cholim of Greater New York, which is affiliated with the Jewish Board of Family and Children's Services. The manual can be purchased from them at 130 East 59th Street, Room 306, New York, NY 10022, (212) 836-1197. In the Greater New York area, the Department of Jewish Family Life Education from the Jewish Board of Family and Children's Services offers training to synagogues and agencies.

*Acts of Loving-Kindness: A Training Manual for Bikkur Holim*, by Rabbi Nancy Flam, Janet Offel, and Rabbi Amy Eilberg, is published through the National Center for Jewish Healing and can be purchased from them at the National Center for Jewish Healing, c/o JBFCS, 120 W. 57th Street, New York, NY 10019, (212-632-4705). It is a written form of the *bikur cholim* training program developed by Rabbis Nancy Flam and Amy Eilberg at *Ruach Ami: The Bay Area Jewish Healing Center in San Francisco*. They worked with numerous synagogues in San Francisco to develop this structured program to help volunteers understand the meaning of *bikur cholim* as "an act of loving-kindness in which God's presence is manifested."

*Give Me Your Hand: Traditional and Practical Guidance on Visiting the Sick*, by Jane Handler and Kim Hetherington with Rabbi Stuart Kelman, was written as a result of a symposium on *bikur cholim* at Temple Adas Israel in Washington, DC, to honor a congregant who had died of cancer in 1986. The purpose was to allow the congregation to address concerns about performing the sometimes difficult and stressful *mitzvah* of *bikur cholim*. In a later edition (1997) Rabbi Stuart Kelman contributed to the book as well. As mentioned previously in suggested books to read, it is a brief but comprehensive guide to understanding the purpose of *bikur cholim* and the do's and don'ts of the actual process. At the conclusion there are thoughts on the topic by several well-known rabbis of various sects. It can be ordered from the National Center for Jewish Healing at the address listed previously or from Congregation Netivot Shalom, 1841 Berkeley Way, Berkeley, CA 94703.

It is important to understand what the aims of *bikur cholim* are in order to recognize the do's and don'ts of the process. When we perform *bikur cholim*, we cannot fix the situation, remove the patient's illness, or even alleviate the illness. *Bikur cholim* cannot alter the patient's feelings.

So why is *bikur cholim* valuable? What does it do?

There are several benefits that result from the mission of *bikur cholim*. Volunteers can comfort a patient. Volunteers can help take away the loneliness that the homebound, nursing home, or hospitalized patient experiences. Volunteers can give the patient a sense of belonging to the community and can help the patient regain a sense of Jewishness. Volunteers may bring in mementos of various Jewish holidays as they are occurring and thereby connect the patient back to the heritage from which he was removed. Volunteers can give the patient back a sense of identity and individuality by taking time to just be there and listen to the patient's story. Volunteers can provide humor and entertainment by using their talents to help alleviate some of the patient's boredom. Volunteers can also help a patient deal with stress and work through the tensions of the illness by being an objective listener while guiding patients to express their feelings. Volunteers can advocate for the patient. By monitoring the patient's condition, volunteers can inform medical staff of any deterioration in health or mental health and of any specific needs expressed by the patient.

Volunteers obtain personal rewards from the process, too. Besides feeling good about being of help to others, volunteers gain a better understanding of life and the stages of life that we go through. By performing *bikur cholim*, they also make a statement about their reverence for life. They learn to appreciate their own good health and also that of their families and are able to realize that if they should ever be in the role of patient, it is important to accept other volunteers who desire to do for them what they have done for others. They gain an interesting understanding of firsthand experiences in history (especially in cases in which they deal with the elderly). They learn more about people in general.

In order to achieve these benefits, there are skills we use to help us become effective *bikur cholim* volunteers. The do's and don'ts will now be discussed in the following areas of *bikur cholim*: The Preparation for the Visit, Entering the Room, and the Introduction (Asking permission to Visit and Getting Settled into Position for the Visit), The Visit (Active Listening, Fully Attentive, Being Nonjudgmental, Dealing with Silence, Directive Questioning, Offering Prayer), the Departure, and After the Departure.

## PREPARATION FOR THE VISIT

A key factor is the importance of allowing the patient to be prepared for the visit, if that is possible. You are a guest, and patients feel more comfortable having guests at certain times when they are able to do their best to accept guests in a dignified manner. For example, visits early in the morning or late at night may be very inappropriate. In the early morning patients may be slow in the process of awakening, getting washed, taking medications, and freshening up for the day. Late at night they may be too tired to receive visitors. Patients with digestive disorders or contagious diseases may not be able to entertain guests in a dignified manner. Also, patients who have headaches, when the noise and the attempt to be a good host are too difficult, should not have visits. For them at this time, a note or a brief telephone call may be sufficient to let the patient know that our thoughts are with him.

A visit on the day of a scheduled surgery may be difficult for a patient because the anxiety he feels may not allow him to be a good host. Also, nurses may be there to prepare him, and a visitor may be more of a burden at that time.

An issue for the volunteer to deal with is comfort. Should the volunteer visit a person the visitor doesn't like but who is ill? The answer to that depends, first, on the comfort of the patient and, second, on the comfort of the volunteer. It may not be beneficial to visit a patient who thinks, "Now that I am sick and not able to function well, this person with whom I've argued can gloat over my misfortunes." Yet it could be beneficial if a visit makes the patient feel that others, including even those he does not like and who do not like him, care enough about him to express concern. Perhaps a phone call ahead of time by the volunteer, asking permission to visit, could help assess this situation.

What about certain prejudices that the volunteer may have? Does the volunteer, for example, have a prejudgment about an AIDS patient? If the volunteer cannot treat the patient fairly and with dignity, then the volunteer should look for a different match, since neither the patient nor the volunteer will benefit. Too often, when a volunteer is uncomfortable, he will show signs of this that the patient may pick up on. For example, one volunteer could not deal with the patient's wasting away as he was dying from AIDS. The volunteer came into the room, stood by the patient's bed, looked out the window or around the room as he spoke, kept interrupting whatever the patient said to him, and kept saying that things would probably be okay in the end. The volunteer did not smile. His face seemed to be frozen in a frown. The patient felt discouraged and depressed by his visitor's demeanor of gloom. Finally, the patient said nothing. The volunteer could not stand the silence and made an excuse to leave. The patient later commented to his nurse: "I don't understand why this visitor came to see me. I'm sorry that he felt so uncomfortable and that there was nothing I could do to make him feel at ease. I wanted to offer him a prayer for his well-being but he wasn't even listening to what I said."

It is also important to think about the patient's comfort. For example, a visitor should not wear perfume or aftershave lotion because someone who is ill may be hypersensitive to smell.

Dress appropriately. Don't look as if you're about to go to the beach for a day of sand and fun while the ill person is stuck in a hospital.

A visitor should think beforehand about what to say. It is important not to stress the patient by bringing bad news. Instead, think of positive conversation openers. There are various possibilities. Perhaps you can quote some applicable poetry or a biblical passage, if that is something the patient would like. If you would like to bring something to give to the patient, bring a newspaper to help him connect to the outside world or a book with positive stories or poems or with Jewish themes to help him connect to the Jewish community, or a craft that you might help the patient create now or leave for the patient to do in her spare time. For example, it might help to leave a book of Jewish humor, anecdotes, or inspiration.

Preparing for the visit often brings a sense of discomfort to the volunteer. As was shown previously by the example of the AIDS patient who felt that he had failed in not being able to comfort the person who was supposed to comfort him, if a volunteer is not comfortable his behavior will often reveal that to the patient. Of course, as is true with any human interaction, one cannot know exactly what is going to happen until put in the situation, but by coming in with some sense of preparation the volunteer at least starts out with a sense of ease.

## ENTERING THE ROOM AND THE INTRODUCTION

Before entering a patient's room, a visitor should knock and ask permission to enter. This makes the volunteer different from the staff of doctors and nurses who, because of hospital and professional rules, take control of the patient. Part of the role of the volunteer, as stated previously, is to show respect to the patient, to allow him some dignity and individuality, and to give him some control in areas such as social functioning. The patient is the host. The volunteer is the guest. By knocking and asking permission to enter, the volunteer allows the patient to make the choice in a respectful way of whether or not he is up to having a visitor. It also allows the patient, who may want a visitor but may feel that at the moment he is not dressed appropriately, to ask for a few minutes so that he can dress to receive visitors.

If a volunteer comes, and there are several visitors present already, he should wait outside until a few people leave, if he has time. If the volunteer cannot wait, he could let the patient know he is there to check on his well-being and that, since the patient is well attended with visitors, he will return another day. Of course, if doctors or other staffpersons are attending to the patient's medical needs, the volunteer cannot interfere with this.

When the volunteer is granted permission to enter, it is important for him to greet the patient. If this is the first visit, the volunteer must give his name and explain his position—that he is a volunteer and what agency he represents. If he already knows the patient, the greeting can be simply verbal, with "Hello, how are you" or a handshake, if appropriate. It is important to address the patient by name. That conveys respect for him as an individual with a specific identity.

The volunteer needs to be aware of nonverbal cues. If a volunteer walks into a room and holds his arms to his chest, this is a type of closure. The message conveyed is that I came to ask you how you are and to give a brief hello. I don't have the time to be here for too long, or I'm not really comfortable being here. This is almost like a dutiful visit. It is important to maintain an open posture to convey the message "I'm here to be with you. Open up to me. Let me hear what's on *your* mind. Tell me *your* story."

Other nonverbal cues include eye contact. Not making eye contact seems to send a message minimizing the importance of the patient to the volunteer. Yet too much eye contact may also be detrimental. It may make patients feel as if the volunteer is staring into the depths of their souls.

Also, body motions such as shaking one's leg, tapping one's foot, or jiggling keys are distractors. They make it seem to the patients that the volunteer is physically here but is not fully attentive to them. It's hard enough to pour out one's heart in the first place, but when the volunteer does not seem to be listening with full attention, why bother to even try?

Storytelling is an art that we all have. A story serves to validate the person telling his story. It is unique. No one else has his story to tell. It allows the patient to give something to his visitor. It also allows the patient to leave his history behind for others so that if he is no longer there, he will be remembered by others because his life does have some importance. His story will teach others about life and will connect them to past generations. It sometimes takes a bit of effort to locate a patient's "master stories," those events in their lives that most characteristically define them. You can try to find those stories by telling some of your own or by asking something like, "Who was the most interesting friend you ever had?" or "When were you the happiest?" Many people like to tell stories about their families, including their parents and their children and grandchildren.

Even young children who are patients have stories to tell. They may be active at times, but sitting down to listen to a story usually helps them in several ways. Telling stories usually has a calming effect by affording them time to actually sit down and relax. It may be a teaching device. Through stories, we learn about other people and other cultures. If the story is biographical, it may help us to know more about the person telling the story. This can serve to connect the listener to the storyteller. For example, when a grandmother tells her granddaughter about the parade she had at her synagogue on Simchat Torah, marching down the block with a flag that had an apple on top, the granddaughter is able to see that her grandmother was a child like her at one time and has not always been a silver-haired old lady.

So, stories are gifts given to us even as young children. The patient, by allowing us to hear his story, is offering us his gift. As a *bikur cholim* volunteer, the compassion we can give is to listen attentively and fully to this story that is being offered. A patient expends a great deal of energy telling his story. An effective volunteer will try to minimize any distractions and give the patient the gift of effective listening. It is important that the volunteer, for example, comes at a time when she will not be in a hurry and can give adequate time to listen, at a time when she will not be hungry and preoccupied by needing to get food, at a time when her health is okay and she will not be preoccupied with pain. It is important for the volunteer to try not to be distracted by her own fears of illness or death or prejudices.

An excellent booklet, titled *Bikur Cholim and Storytelling: A New Approach to Visiting the Sick in Hospitals, Nursing Homes and the Homebound* by Murray Nossel, talks about the importance of the story and effective listening skills to help the *bikur cholim* volunteer. It is published by the Bikur Cholim Coordinating Council of Greater New York and can be purchased through them at the address given previously.

There is a term called *posture of involvement*. It shows the patient that the volunteer is focused exclusively on him and his issues and indicates a readiness to listen. The volunteer faces the patient squarely, close to eye level; maintains a fair amount of eye contact; and leans forward toward the patient. These are cues to the patient of being here ready to listen and to become involved.

Sometimes a patient will ask the volunteer to have a seat. The volunteer should not sit on the bed because that cuts into the patient's space and can cause discomfort to him if he feels obligated to stay in one position to not disturb his visitor. If possible, the volunteer should pull up a chair next to the bed and set it facing the patient so that eye contact can be made. We normally have a comfortable distance in a social encounter, in which it is neither too close and overwhelming nor so far that one loses comfortable eye contact and hearing ability. A visitor should adhere to requests from the patient as well; for example, a patient who is hard of hearing may ask his visitor to sit a little closer.

Sometimes there are distracting factors in the environment that may detract from the importance of the visit. Distractions may cause patients to be unable to appreciate the visit as a source of comfort. For example, a window view may take away from the focus being on the patient. Perhaps the curtains could be drawn. Perhaps the door needs to be shut if it is too noisy in the hall. The volunteer should always ask the patient's permission to do so and ask in such a way as to show that the volunteer is interested in focusing on the patient. For example, one might say, "It seems to be so noisy in the hall. Would you like me to shut the door so that I can hear better what *you* have to say?"

## THE VISIT

Now that you are with the patient, have made your introduction, and have settled into a comfortable position of involvement, you are ready to participate in the visit.

It is understandable that doubts may emerge at this point. It is common, for example, for new volunteers to ask themselves, "What can I say?" or "What if I say the wrong thing?" These are key questions that most volunteers have at one time or another, and too often they are used as an excuse for not volunteering. If we understand the purpose of *bikur cholim*—to examine the situation and do what needs to be done to comfort the patient—then we may have less anxiety regarding what to do and say. We are looking to say and do that which will comfort the patient.

Following are some examples of what may be said when a volunteer begins the visit. They will then be accompanied by an explanation regarding their appropriateness.

The volunteer comes into the room and asks the patient about her illness. The patient reports the name of her disease, and the volunteer says that her mother had died of that disease, but there have been many advances in medication since then.

If we think about the aim of *bikur cholim*, it becomes self-evident that linking death to this illness might frighten the patient at a time when she needs all the support and positive thoughts she can get. If the patient wanted to talk to an objective person about her situation, just to sort out her feelings, she is not as likely to feel able to talk after the scare that people die from this illness has just been planted in her mind.

In another situation, the volunteer comes into the room and asks the patient about her illness. After the patient gives its name and some symptoms, the volunteer says, "It just takes time and rest. You'll see, in a few days you'll be feeling better. By Rosh Hashannah you'll be home and able to go to synagogue."

The volunteer means well and wants to convey a positive attitude to the patient to make her feel better. We are usually able to recognize when someone is saying something just to be nice, but

64

sometimes this false situation (since it is obvious that the volunteer is not God and has no say in determining the outcome of the illness) cheats the patient out of doing something that in the end might really bring her comfort. This volunteer is making light of the feelings of despair that the patient is really experiencing, and now there is no way she can talk about this to a volunteer who will not be able to listen objectively. The patient is not likely to continue to tell her story to someone who, it seems, will not really understand what she is trying to say and probably will continue to make light of things by telling her that all is right when it isn't.

The patient reveals to the volunteer that the staff is not attentive to him, that he has to wait to be helped with washing up in the morning, that the doctors run in for one minute and give him a quick checkup and then leave before he can ask any questions, and that the food is tasteless. The volunteer replies that this hospital has a reputation for constantly making people wait before anything gets done. Perhaps they are short-staffed and should hire more nurses and aides. This is a teaching hospital, so, of course, the doctors also have students to attend to, and their time is limited.

Volunteers may feel they are being supportive by agreeing with the patient on issues such as these. What is happening instead is that by joining in the criticism, the volunteer is sending the message that any doubts the patient may have had about his medical care may be valid. If a patient does not have faith in his doctor, he may become more upset about his care, and positive mental health and being in good spirits play a major part in helping a patient deal with his illness.

The aim of *bikur cholim* is to find ways to help the patient to be able to talk about his concerns—to express what he feels the situation to be, to vent his anger, to sort out his feelings, to understand his options, to come to terms with what these options are, and perhaps to select options when he has a choice. These examples show how a well-meaning volunteer may unwittingly inhibit a patient from taking an action that could ultimately be of comfort to him. Using the same examples, we can explore what the volunteer might have done instead to enable the patient to begin to talk.

In regard to the situation where the patient tells the volunteer about her illness, the volunteer could say: "It sounds like it has not been easy for you to be in the hospital. Would you like to tell me more about what it is like to have this illness and to be here?" or "It seems like this is hard for you! Are you comfortable? Can I perhaps adjust your pillow to make you more comfortable?" or "Sounds like there are many changes for you! I was just noticing those photos on the wall. Are those of family members?" or "I see that you have a *Siddur* here. Would you like me to say a prayer for you or read a psalm?"

These suggestions will: (1) Affirm to the patient that the volunteer recognizes there is a problem or hardship for the patient in being ill. In the event that being in a hospital or nursing home is not a problem, the volunteer will still come across as someone who is understanding and empathetic. The statement was phrased in terms of "it seems like." That just means that the volunteer interpreted it that way, but through further dialogue the patient can further explain herself and her issue. As for example, she may say, "By being in the hospital, I am getting better care than at home because I live alone and both my daughters live far away." Then that can lead to further dialogue with the patient, perhaps this time about her two daughters. (2) Show that the volunteer is not being judgmental and is not making a diagnosis. The volunteer does not say the illness is very serious and sure to cause death. The volunteer is not giving a positive prognosis, either. It is obvious that the patient may report her illness as one thing, but that there may be more to her illness than she is actually talking about. Therefore, a volunteer really does not have all the facts and medical knowledge to even be capable of making a diagnosis and should refrain from doing so. (3). Use a statement that focuses on the patient and attempts to involve her in talking about herself. This serves two purposes. First, it shows the patient that the volunteer is talking specifically about her and is attempting to know *her* special story. Second, it opens up areas for talk.

The focus of a *bikur cholim* session should be on patients and their issues, not on volunteers. That is why the introduction of the volunteer is usually brief: "My name is Sharon, and I am a volunteer representing North Shore Jewish Center. I came to see how you are feeling." After the introduction, the focus then goes to the patient and her illness. "It must be difficult for you to be in the hospital and away from your home."

The volunteer is then ready to direct questions toward the patient to get her to speak about her situation. The volunteer is attempting to comfort the patient by focusing full attention on her and requesting her to tell her issues and *her* story.

How does the volunteer do this effectively?

There are several key factors involved in the communication process. Once the patient has started talking and telling her story, the aim of the volunteer should be to give the patient full attention, not to distract her so she can feel comfortable in continuing, not to minimize what she has to say, to be supportive of her issues, and to accept the patient as she is without being judgmental. By doing these things the volunteer validates the patient as an important part of society, even though her hospitalization has removed her from her usual housing and from the Jewish community. Some of these techniques that serve to encourage the patient to continue with her story include: Active Listening, Door Openers, Minimal Encouragers, Open-Ended Questions, Paraphrasing, Reflecting Back Feelings, Silence, and Prayer.

## Active Listening

This process includes looking at the patient at eye level; leaning toward her; keeping one's arms in an open, comfortable position; making the environment as non-distracting as possible; interrupting as little as possible; and responding minimally to show that you are listening (sometimes with nonverbal gestures, such as nodding your head in agreement, and sometimes with words, such as "yes," "right," "I see," and "uh huh"). Remember, your aim is not to compete with the speaker for attention. If you compare war stories, it takes away from the importance of what she has to say, and her story no longer becomes her story when diffused by your interruptions and interjections about you. The patient's story is unique and needs to be seen that way in order for her to feel comfortable about proceeding. If you tell her that you already know her story because of your similar experience, then she doesn't need to repeat a story you already know. You are not visiting the patient to tell your story. In many ways, as a *bikur cholim* volunteer you are the patient's therapist and support. As a result of the visit she sees that others care about her, and if she feels comfortable she will tell you her story. You don't have to be a doctor or a therapist by profession in order for this to occur. You have to show genuine interest in her, and she will proceed.

Dr. Raymond Stovich, a psychologist in the San Francisco Bay Area who helps train *bikur cholim* volunteers, illustrates this with a story about Elisabeth Kubler-Ross who, as mentioned earlier, has written about the stages a dying person goes through in dealing with a terminal diagnosis. She was working with dying patients at the University of Chicago Hospital to find ways to help her patients. Sometimes it was very difficult. She went back after visiting hours to see a man who was dying of cancer. She noticed that he was talking to someone so she did not enter. She could hear the man pouring out deep thoughts and feelings to his visitor. She waited for the visitor to come out so she could discover the secret to accomplishing what she had been trying, but with little success, to do for this patient. She was amazed when the visitor exiting the room turned out to be the cleaning lady. She asked the cleaning lady what she had done to achieve this amazing feat. "The cleaning lady responded quite simply, 'Honey, I didn't do a thing. I guess he just knew I was willing to listen. And when he started to talk I just sat there, held his hand and listened to him. The good Lord did all the rest!"

This story was found in *Acts of Loving-Kindness: A Training Manual For Bikkur Holim*. It clearly illustrates that *bikur cholim* is a skill from the heart, and we are all capable of performing that.

A volunteer came to see Richard S., who was recovering from a stroke and was paralyzed on his left side. She asked him how he was feeling, and Richard stated that he had never been sick before in his life, so this was hard for him. The volunteer stated that she knew what he meant. She knew what he must be feeling, for she also had been a basically healthy person until two years ago when she had found a lump on her breast. It had resulted in her going into this very hospital to have it removed. After her surgery she had three months of chemotherapy, and then everything was all right.

Richard replied that he was glad that she had done well, and then he turned to talking about the weather and thanked her for taking the time to visit with him.

The volunteer was well-meaning. She used her own story to interrupt Richard when he was about to reveal his story. She meant to make him see that she understood him because she had undergone a similar experience, and it had worked out well for her. He was polite and listened to her story. But her interruption took away from the importance and uniqueness of his story. To him, it no longer became a story worth telling.

Hirschel G. told the volunteer that he had been hospitalized for a broken arm and a broken hip due to a recent fall. He also has a lump at the back of his head. He seemed withdrawn and did not smile. When the volunteer had asked if she could visit, he grumpily said, "I guess, if that's what you want to do." The volunteer replied that it sounded like he has been going through a very difficult time. He talked about the recent death of his wife, to whom he had been married for fifty-six years. They lived in the house where he still lives. His wife used to cook for him and keep the house immaculate. Four months ago she had a fatal heart attack, dying in the ambulance on the way to the emergency room. The patient revealed that he missed his wife so much. It was hard for him to live alone in the big house with no one there to talk to and no one to share a meal with. He was not used to cooking for himself.

As he said these things, the volunteer thought about her own grandparents. Her grandfather had died about a year ago and had left her grandmother alone, with many hardships and much loneliness. She did not say anything about this to Hirschel but instead listened carefully as he talked. Occasionally, she would interject some phrases like "I see," "What did you do next?," "Are there any neighbors who could help?," "That certainly sounds difficult," "uh huh." Everything the volunteer said encouraged the patient to go on with his story. She was actually saying to Hirschel: "I hear your story," "I am interested in what you have to say," "I don't know your unique story. Tell me more."

Hirschel continued with his story by explaining that his present hardships were a result of his wife's death, and then he talked about his wife and their relationship. He had not talked about her very much after the death and found it helpful to tell his story. It was something he needed to do to begin the process of grieving for her, and the volunteer, by actively listening, was enabling him to do this.

When, after an hour's visit, the volunteer announced that she had to leave to be home for her children's school bus, he thanked her for the visit and asked if she would come again. She replied that she would come back the following Tuesday, which is the day she normally volunteers, and she did return as promised to listen to more of his story.

## Responses to the Patient's Story

Once the patient starts his story, how does the volunteer show continued interest in what he has to say? How does the volunteer encourage him to continue with his story? A lot depends on effective responses from the volunteer, which help the volunteer stay out of the patient's way and which encourage the patient to keep going. The following are some of these skills:

### Door Openers

These statements invite patients in a noncoercive way to speak. Examples are "How are you?" and "May I talk to you?" They invite patient to talk and allow him to choose whether he is up to having a visitor. One should then try to ask questions that cannot be answered with a simple "yes" or "no" but that instead open up a conversation. An ill librarian, for example, could be asked about which were the most popular books among readers.

A patient who is willing to have a visitor can begin to talk about his illness and symptoms and how they have affected him. A patient who does not want a visitor can politely say that he does not feel up to a visit at the moment because he needs to get some rest. The patient has made the choice regarding having a visitor, and the volunteer need not feel rejected if the patient does not choose to see him at this time.

## Minimal Encouragers

These statements do not let the volunteer get in the way of what the patient has to say, and at the same time they serve to let the patient know that the volunteer has become involved in listening to his story and is requesting him to continue with it. The volunteer does not make a judgment, give advice, or interrupt by sharing similar personal incidents.

Appropriate minimal encouragers might be: "You were saying!," "Right!," "Yes," "Uh huh!," "Then what happened?," or "How does it make you feel?"

It is inappropriate to distract attention from the story by such statements as "I think" or "When that happened to me . . ."

For example, when one patient talked about hating to be in this hospital because the doctors never stay long enough to answer questions, one volunteer replied that she had been hospitalized here once and felt the same way. The patient stopped the flow of his story and went off to vent about how unfair that ·was, and the rest of the visit digressed into opinions about poor treatment.

A similar comment was made to another volunteer. This volunteer recognized that the patient needed to continue on with his feeling that the doctors were not treating him in the most effective way. Her reply was "How does that make you feel?" She did not interrupt the issue he wanted to discuss and kept her comment focused on him. The visit ended with his deciding to write down ahead of time any questions he had so that he could present them to the doctor. The volunteer had guided the patient to find a solution.

## Open-Ended Questions

These questions help direct the patient's thinking. They allow and encourage the patient to talk about what is on his mind. Questions should be asked one at a time. They should not be questions that can be answered with simple "yes" or "no" but rather should suggest topics that the patient may have an interest in speaking about. They will give him ideas of where to direct his story. A "why" question is not usually advised, because it may make the patient feel that you are making a judgment about something, that you are questioning his reasoning or authority. On the other hand, a "how" question has the effect of making the patient feel that he is an authority and can teach you something that you have made a request to learn about.

For example, one volunteer came to visit a patient she had known for several weeks. She greeted the patient and then asked her if she was feeling better today than she had been feeling at the time of the last visit. The patient replied that she was better today and thus answered the question quickly.

Another volunteer greeted her patient and asked how she was feeling today. The patient replied that she had had a bad headache for the last three days, but that it was much better today. She said she believed that the weather had something to do with making her sinuses bad, and as a result she got headaches. She also talked about having a lot of family pressures and said she felt they contributed to bringing on her headaches.

The volunteer's reply, in an attempt to keep the conversation going, was another question directed at the patient. "What kinds of family pressures are happening?"

The patient replied: "My daughter and her husband are constantly fighting. I'm afraid they are going to split up. Their children are going to have a hard time if that happens. They are so young. They are only seven and three. Last time they were fighting, I took the kids to my house. Now I'm here in the hospital, and I can't shelter them from the tensions."

The volunteer shook her head and said: "It certainly sounds difficult for everyone involved. Is there something you can think of that has helped in the past?"

"Yes," replied the patient. "You know, last year when this happened they spoke with our rabbi, and he was very helpful. He persuaded them to go to marriage counseling, and that worked for a little while. Actually, I think they really do get along better now. It is just that my son-in-law lost his job last month, so there's lots of tensions due to limited income."

The volunteer replied, "I see! Do you have any ideas about how they can alleviate some of these financial tensions?"

"Yes, as a matter of fact, I do. Of course, my son-in-law is searching daily for work by putting in a lot of applications. He does have some specialized training in accounting, and tax season is coming soon. I am sure that he will get some work soon.

"Talking about this with you has allowed me to see that what I was really afraid of—the marriage splitting up because they just do not get along—is not the true problem. I know they love each other, and it is just normal tensions that are responsible for their fighting. It makes me feel better that the financial tensions will eventually be solved, and I feel confident that my daughter and son-in-law will be together when my three-year-old grandson is called to the Torah to celebrate his *Bar Mitzvah*."

The volunteer, by showing continued interest in her patient, by not being judgmental, by not interjecting her own thoughts and feelings, and by asking open-ended questions one at a time, was able to direct the patient toward solving her own problem.

Sometimes we get helpful advice from patients who want to tell us about living skills that have helped them in the past and that they feel will be helpful to us. Independently, two patients in a nursing home gave me the same advice. When our topic got on to dirty laundry and the inability to get socks white, each separately advised me that they used to soak their socks and soiled white laundry in the Efferdent tablets that they normally use for cleaning dentures. I figured that if two experienced people revealed the same secret, then there must be some validity to it. I didn't even have to purchase the product since my daughter, who was wearing an orthodontic retainer at that time, already had a supply of Efferdent to clean her device. I tried the secret procedure, and having soiled white socks is now past history in our family. When I thanked my nursing home residents, both felt happy to have been of help and since then have felt free to offer other helpful hints, some of which have worked well, while others were too antiquated to be of help. But I always thank them, which validates their helpfulness and makes them feel that they are useful and appreciated even though they are no longer able to live in the outside community.

### Paraphrasing

This technique focuses on content. Its purpose is to allow the patient to see that you are listening to what he is saying. When you repeat in your own words what you understand him to have said, he can say, "Yes, that is what I have said," or he can clarify it to help you understand better. In either case, it shows the patient that you are interested.

For example, the patient stated that he was well cared for in the hospital, that he gets three meals and is bathed daily. At home he finds it hard to shop for food and cook unless his daughter helps him with these chores. Sometimes a neighbor comes as well and brings meals to him.

The volunteer paraphrased this as follows: "It sounds like living alone is hard for you and that you have to depend on family and friends to do things for you because you don't get around on your own so well."

"That's right! I used to drive wherever I wanted to go, but now I have cataracts on both eyes and don't see well enough to drive."

In my own *bikur cholim* work, I used to be uncomfortable when a patient who had a stroke or was on a ventilator would try to say something to me that I was unable, because of the effects of the illness, to comprehend. The patient is usually aware of the problem, since I am not the first person who has had trouble understanding what he means to say. I find that often a little patience pays off. My first step is to try to repeat what I believe the patient is saying. Then he usually acknowledges whether I am correct. If I am incorrect, he tries again to communicate. I usually feel comfortable enough to state that sometimes it takes time, but I can try again. Sometimes we resort to pen and paper or to calling out letters of the alphabet to spell words. Of utmost importance is patience. That communicates to the patient: "You are important. I am here to focus my attention on you." I also find that as time goes on and I get to know a patient, I can understand him better.

One of my most meaningful *bikur cholim* experiences was with a ninety-four-year-old man whom I visited weekly for two years until his death. Because he was on a respirator, I had trouble understanding what he verbalized, so we rarely had long conversations. Because he was paralyzed, he was unable to use nonverbal communication such as pointing. He did like human touch and would occasionally say a few words, which, as I got to know him better, I learned to understand. Sometimes he would tell me to comb his hair, sometimes rub his neck or feet, and other times stroke his forehead. He had been hospitalized for over two years before I was introduced to him by a hospital social worker, who was keen enough to realize that in spite of the fact that he could not ask for it, he, too, had a need for human contact. His family was also wise enough to leave a story he had written about his volunteer work in a fire department in the small town where he had grown up and still lived until his hospitalization. He had been honored for seventy-five years of volunteer work there. Nearly every week he would ask me to read his story to him. I looked forward to sharing his story and felt honored that he invited me to do this every time we met. He had a wife who was in her eighties

75

and a younger brother who was close to ninety. Because they lived about forty-five minutes from the hospital, they were unable to get there daily to visit. He had three children who came whenever they were able, but in general, he was without visitors for whole days or a good portion of the day. The family did, however, try to leave things that were a part of him and that could help him keep his connection to his outside community and to the Jewish community. The story he wrote about the fire department was one example. Also, every holiday they would bring some kind of symbol of the holiday to share with him, such as a Chanukah *menorah* that had light bulbs. Although we did not communicate verbally, our visits, with my paraphrasing what this patient seemed to be asking me to do and acting on it, were valuable for both of us. The patient would smile as I came into his room and said hello. I would often get warm feelings within my soul. These feelings are hard to describe in words, but somehow I got a sense deep within me that my grief for my father, who had died when I was fourteen, was finally being worked through as I found myself able to care for others who are sick and dying.

*Reflecting Back Feelings*

People also need to deal with feelings in order to energize themselves for taking action. This task is a little more difficult at times for the *bikur cholim* volunteer. It is easy to paraphrase content, as was discussed in the previous section, because it involves working with what is verbalized. Feelings are sometimes not verbalized, or what is verbalized may be incongruent with what the person is truly feeling inside. If we think about a situation in which a friend, for example, is wearing an outfit that we feel is truly ugly, we can understand this concept easier. Perhaps the friend asks us how we like her new outfit. We might be honest and tell her we hate it, but more likely we will be kinder and either blatantly lie and tell her how wonderful she looks or find some happy medium to soften our intense feelings of distaste. A difficulty in bending the truth is that it may be detected by someone who knows us because our tone of voice, posture, or facial expressions may betray us. A flat, unexcited tone from a friend who is not normally flat and without affect communicates more than the actual content of what is said. A volunteer came to visit Miriam A., an eighty-year-old homebound woman, and asked her how she was feeling. Miriam stated that she was well, but the volunteer noticed that she was pale and that while she was talking, she would sigh involuntarily. The volunteer sensed that something was bothering Miriam but could not tell if the cause was physical or mental tensions. He tried to direct Miriam toward expressing her feelings by asking her questions and reflecting back what he sensed her feelings might be.

"Miriam, are you feeling tired today? Your face seems to be more pale than usual."

"No, I slept the same amount of hours that I usually do. But I do remember having a dream about my husband. I know he has been dead for five years already, and I should be used to his not being here. I guess the dream was so real that when I woke up, I expected to find him there, and he wasn't." She sighed as she said that.

The volunteer reflected back to her that it must be disappointing to have expected him to be there and to find that he wasn't.

Miriam replied: "I feel so depressed!" Tears came to her eyes briefly. Then she began to tell her visitor about how she had met her husband, and how in the beginning she had not liked him because he was not as good-looking as the boy she had a crush on. Then she related some adventurous stories about how he had chased after her to try to win her affections. One of her girlfriends, who felt that the two were a great match, even plotted with him to set up a meeting at the synagogue. The friend invited her to a Sisterhood meeting at the synagogue, and when she got there, there was no meeting—but there he was.

She laughed as she relayed some fond memories. In the end she told the volunteer that it felt good to talk about these memories. She seemed less depressed, and she said that she realized that someday, when God was ready, she would be reunited with her husband, but for now she had some projects to do, one of these being knitting an afghan for the baby her son and daughter-in-law are expecting in another month.

The volunteer told her that he found her story very interesting and could relate some of her experiences to the present. Perhaps he learned that human nature never really changes.

## Silence

Sometimes a volunteer will visit a patient who is not ready to tell his story or one who has started his story but has stopped in the middle with a period of silence. Silence is often the most uncomfortable situation a volunteer can be put in. The fear of wondering what one should say is magnified when there is no response on the other end. A volunteer often feels uncomfortable giving a monologue to someone who does not even acknowledge wanting to listen, to someone who in all likelihood is already preoccupied with his own thoughts. This sometimes makes a volunteer respond by looking for an excuse to say goodbye and exit as soon as possible.

But initiating and maintaining human contact, human presence, shows true compassion. It is the true meaning of *bikur cholim* to assess the situation and just to be there. Whether the patient's silence is due to physical or psychological reasons, a patient who feels that others care seems to thrive longer. Perhaps at this time the patient is going through a traumatic issue and telling his story has brought it to the surface. He needs time to compose himself and to think. The volunteer could offer her hand to the patient as an indication of being there and offering support. The volunteer's job is not to make the patient change his feelings. It is, however, to give him support as he tries to deal with these feelings. Also, it is crucial to remember that some people are very private. They want and need to keep their feelings to themselves. They resent some stranger asking them about their private lives. Such privacy needs to be respected. In such cases, a simple hello is sufficient.

Even in cases when patients are in a coma, being present and holding the dying patient's hand seems to provide some form of comfort.

The volunteer listened attentively as Jacob spoke about the upcoming holiday. Pesach would begin in a week, and his doctors had indicated that he would probably be home for the first *seder*. Usually, he was the one responsible for leading it. His wife loves to cook and has already made plans to have it at their house for their son, daughter-in-law, and three grandchildren. He stopped and became silent.

The volunteer commented that talking about Passover seemed to be stressful to him.

He nodded his head and was silent once again.

The volunteer asked if she could hold his hand, and he accepted. She stroked his hand as he sat in silence.

After about fifteen minutes, he revealed to her that Passover was hard for him because it brought back memories of the first night of Passover when he was twenty years old and was going to lead the family *seder* for the first time. He was excited about leading the *seder*, but it never happened because on that afternoon his younger sister, to whom he was really close, was killed in a car accident. He talked a little more about his sister and their relationship and thanked the volunteer for staying. He said he had not talked about the death in many years since he didn't want to burden family with his feelings.

Besides the listening skills discussed here, there are also other activities that the volunteer might offer a patient.

## Prayer

Prayer is an essential part of *bikur cholim*. In many synagogues, at a *Shabbat* service members will come up to the *Bimah* to state the name of a person who is ill so that a *Mi Sheberach* (blessing) could be said for specific people who are ill, as well as for any others in the community in need of the blessing.

Prayer is a hope. A person may be dying, and hope for recovery may not be realistic, but hope for less physical and less mental pain may be realistic. It could also mean finding comfort in the knowledge that the patient's family will be taken care of and hope that they will find happiness in pursuing their missions in life.

Prayer is done for healing, but in some cases physical healing may not be possible. If physical healing is impossible, mental healing through confession may be possible.

Prayer is a kind of support. It makes a connection between the ill person and the Jewish community, for it shows the patient that even though he is not able to be there physically, he is in the thoughts of community members.

Volunteers often experience anxiety about using prayer while visiting a patient. There are questions about what prayer does. Does it really help a sick person? Does God hear the prayer, and does He have power to heal? How do I know if a person really wants me to pray? If he does agree to prayer, should I pray with him or for him? What's the benefit of a prayer if the person is dying?

If prayer is thought of as reconnection to the Jewish community, then it becomes a spiritual part of the *bikur cholim* process. A complete relationship includes physically being there, showing compassion and understanding by listening and directing with undivided attention, and bringing a sense of spirituality through prayer.

If the prayer is unacceptable to the patient at the time of the visit, or if the volunteer does not feel ready to offer prayer to the patient, then the prayer could be done in an alternate way. An example could be a Mi Sheberach at synagogue or even just a thought or silent prayer done by the volunteer. It could be done as a donation of *tzedakah* to a Jewish cause in the name of the patient. This further links the patient to the Jewish community.

As the volunteer becomes more acquainted with the patient, he may then feel more comfortable offering a prayer in person, and the patient also may feel more comfortable accepting the prayer from someone he knows and who is no longer a stranger. A prayer offered by a friend is usually felt to be sincere. Any combinations of these are acceptable.

Part of the reason we may be hesitant to offer a prayer is that we are unsure of what to say.

The *Siddur* is a rich source of prayer. The traditional prayer for healing is as follows:

> May the one who blessed our ancestors Sarah and Abraham, Rebecca and Isaac, Leah, Rachel and Jacob, bless _____ son/daughter of _____ and _____ along with all the ill among us. Grant insight to those who bring healing; courage and faith to those who are sick; love and strength to us and all who love them. God, let Your spirit rest upon all who are ill and comfort them. May they and we soon know a time of complete healing, a healing of the body and a healing of the spirit, and let us say: Amen.

The volunteer could make up a prayer, by saying something like "I pray for the complete recovery and well-being of_____," or "I pray that _____ will have a healthy and peaceful life."

Some volunteers might feel comfortable offering to read a psalm or an inspirational poem or story. Psalms 23, which was cited in a course I took in pastoral counseling as a basis for *bikur cholim*—that we are all responsible for the well-being of members of our community—is one to consider reading. It is as follows:

> The Lord is my Shepherd. I shall not want. He maketh me to lie down in green pastures: He leadeth me beside still waters. He restoreth my soul; He guideth me in straight paths for His name's sake. Yea, though I walk through the valley of the shadow of death I shall fear no evil, for Thou art with me; Thy rod and Thy staff, they comfort me. Thou preparest a table before me in the presence of mine enemies; Thou anointest my head with oil; my cup runneth over. Surely goodness and mercy shall follow me all the days of my life, and I shall dwell in the house of the Lord forever.

Other volunteers may offer to sit in silence with the patient so they could each pray individually.

I was once asked by the priest at the nursing home where I volunteer to visit a Jewish patient and to say a prayer for him because the rabbi was not available, and I was the Jewish volunteer. The first thought that came to my mind was that probably the priest would be able to do a better job because he knew a lot of prayers by heart. I almost panicked at the thought of being put on the spot to come up with a prayer. But I also felt honored that the priest would seek me out to perform this task. The patient was breathing with the help of an oxygen tank and mask. I asked if I could hold his hand and he nodded in the affirmative. I stroked his hand, and he held on tightly as I said something to him, to the effect that I hoped he would be able to rest easily and be free of pain. Then I held his hand in silence for about an hour. I felt comfortable being there with him to help him feel that he was not all alone, to help him see that he was still a part of the Jewish community by being in our thoughts. I told him I would say a prayer for him at the synagogue, if that was okay with him, and he nodded in the affirmative.

## Touch

An aim of *bikur cholim* is to comfort a patient and make him physically and mentally better. The touch of a hand by a well-meaning friendly person can be a strong connection for the patient to the outside community and it can give him a great deal of comfort to feel a part of his community once again. Touch provides peace and calmness. It is a gesture to show the patient that you will not abandon him.

If the patient is alert and aware, ask for permission to hold his hand. If granted permission, always tell the patient that if at any time he feels uncomfortable and wants you to stop holding his hand or stroking his arm, he should let you know. After all, pleasing the patient and giving comfort is a prime aim of *bikur cholim*.

As a volunteer, I get a good feeling from the sense of touch, too. For me, it is a connection to the hospital, to illness, to old age, all of which I may encounter at some time in the future. It also connects me to my father, and even after more than thirty years since his death, it helps me grieve for him in a positive way. It helps me understand now what I could not comprehend at age fourteen. It allows me to take action to heal.

I remember reading a story in *Chicken Soup for The Woman's Soul*, edited by Jack Canfield and Mark Victor Hansen, a popular bestseller that has many versions and tells true stories that people send in on such topics as love, parenthood, challenges, and so forth. One story that illustrates the importance of touch has frequently remained on my mind. It goes something like this:

A husband and wife had separate rooms in a nursing home. The woman was confined to her bed. Her husband was able to walk around. He visited her throughout the day. At bedtime each night he would come into her room and fluff her pillow and tuck her in. Then he would stroke her hand and give her a big kiss, and she would drift peacefully off to sleep.

One day the husband had a sudden heart attack and passed away. For weeks after his death, the nurse who got her ready for bed noticed that the old woman was restless and had trouble sleeping. Finally, one night the nurse did what her instincts told her to do. She held the woman's hand, stroked it softly for several minutes, and gave the woman a goodnight kiss on her cheek. The old woman seemed much calmer than she had been for a long time and soon fell into a peaceful sleep.

*Activities to Do for the Patient*

These activities include such simple tasks as fluffing pillows or drawing open shades to let the sunshine in. If the visit is to a homebound individual, one could offer to do some household chores, such as wash dishes, do laundry, or cook food. Always ask the patient if the activity is okay to perform. Don't just proceed to do something because you judge it to be needed.

Sometimes patients will request the volunteer to do something for them. If there is any uncertainty about whether the request would be a health problem for the patient, or a liability problem if the patient should fall while you are supervising, check first.

For example, when visiting patients at the hospital, I sometimes get a request that I bring them a cup of coffee from the pantry. I always tell them that I have to check with the nurse to make sure that it is consistent with their diet, and I do ask before acting. If a patient asks me to escort her to the bathroom, I ask the nurse if she is steady enough on her feet for me to do that. If not, I make the nurse aware of the patient's need so that she can ask someone who is trained and properly insured to do the task. I always let the patient know if my position as a volunteer does not allow me to honor the request.

### Activities to Do with the Patient

Besides just talking, there may be some participatory activities to do with the patient. One suggestion is craft activities. These can be good for many reasons. They may be a kind of physical therapy, in that they let the patient use her hands. They may bring back memories of past talents. They result in a product that the patient can keep to display and show off to others or that the patient can give to others as a gift. They may lead to the patient taking up a hobby to keep busy with. While creating the craft object, the patient may remember stories regarding some more of her life experiences.

Another suggestion is letter writing. A patient who is unable to use his hands may want to keep in contact with family members who do not live near enough to visit. As the patient tells the volunteer what to write, this often leads to more stories about how the person you are writing to fits into the family, what that person is like, and what role that person has in the patient's life.

Board games may be a good social experience in a nursing home, which can help residents get to know each other.

Anna, age eighty-seven, always carries a Scrabble game in a bag that is hung over the back of her wheelchair. Because the fingers on her one hand are crippled due to arthritis, and her other hand is bent due to the effects of a stroke, she cannot keep score in a Scrabble game. She eagerly awaits the volunteer's weekly visit to ensure that she can play once a week, and she searches for other volunteers who come sporadically. Whenever she meets a new resident, the first question out of her mouth is: "Do you play Scrabble?"

On Sunday, when her regular volunteer comes, she quickly wheels herself into the dining room to set up the game. She always comments on how she views Scrabble as being good for the mind. Every day she goes to the library to read a book, usually nonfiction, so that she can learn a bit of history and keep up with current events. She also studies the dictionary and tries to learn one or two new words each day.

The volunteer did not realize how important the Scrabble game really was to Anna until one day when a nurse, who was an acquaintance of the volunteer, came to sit and talk as the game was starting. Anna is usually a very polite and friendly woman who makes every effort not to hurt anyone's feelings, but she was angry that the nurse was distracting the volunteer from starting the game. She was unable to contain herself any longer, and she politely said to the nurse: "Aren't you supposed to be back at your station to count your medications?" The nurse took the hint and said goodbye. The two-hour Scrabble game began at last.

The game of Scrabble often became very exciting. Sometimes the volunteer had to be a mediator when players began to squabble over what was and what was not an acceptable word. The volunteer felt sad when Anna placed the word *kvetch* in spaces that would allow her to have triple score for her letters. Unfortunately, the word was just not found in the edition of Webster's dictionary they were using to check their words. Anna sulked for a few minutes when the other player, who was not Jewish, triumphantly challenged her word, but five minutes later she was back to playing the game with enthusiasm.

Another activity might be helping the patient make a family tree or a tape of family stories. Presenting a gift to other family members is an exciting challenge and gives the patient something to live for as he begins to see himself as having an important job to perform. The volunteers task is to help the patient organize his presentation and to evoke from him more and more material. The volunteer is the patient's test audience for the performance of his story. That is why active listening, with minimal interruptions except to guide the plot of the story, is very important. Sometimes, from session to session, it might be good to play back what was taped or to read back what was written just as a review for the patient so he can continue on.

Especially with the elderly or with someone who has short-term memory problems, a license to reminisce is like a lease on life. It sends the message that even though I am not out in the community right now, what I did when I was there has an importance and can be instructive to others who were not there to experience it.

Hyman, age 100, told his volunteer about World War I. He was not in active service but had a job in the Brooklyn Navy Yard as a supervisor. Part of his job was to calculate the amount of concrete that was needed to build roads. He asked the volunteer for a piece of paper and pencil, and with a shaky hand, he showed her how he calculated the amount of cement. His math was quick and accurate. The volunteer thought to herself that modern technology might be valuable, but there were consequences to pay. Her nine-year-old daughter could do these calculations faster than Hyman because she used a calculator, but when it came to understanding how to physically do the math, her skills were way behind Hyman's. Perhaps modern technology makes it too easy to avoid learning basic skills. She hadn't thought about this much before because she had been raised in the in-between generation, when the basics were still being taught, and the calculators came into use a little later.

Another suggestion for an activity to do with a patient is to share a holiday. Minimally, it can be done weekly if the visit is late in the week, around *Shabbat*. There are many ways to share a holiday. One would involve bringing in some of the traditional foods associated with the holiday. But before doing that, the volunteer must check with the hospital or nursing home staff (or

86

family, if it is a homebound visit) to be sure that the food you bring is not harmful, if the patient is on a restricted diet due to health conditions. Another way to share the holiday is to bring symbols of the celebration. For *Shabbat* it would be candles (perhaps the kind with light bulbs could be left with the patient for the holiday), a *Siddur*, a *tallit* and *kippah* for a man, a challah cover and challah, a book of Psalms. The volunteer could share some of the service with the patient and read and discuss the portion of the Torah for the week. Perhaps the volunteer and patient could sing some holiday songs.

Holiday themes are excellent for group visits to adult and nursing homes. One family from a synagogue did a *Tu' bishvat seder* for twelve Jewish residents at a predominantly non-Jewish nursing home. The volunteers included the husband and wife and their two young daughters, ages four and six, and four other members of the synagogue who were also willing to come. A plate was prepared with a variety of dried and fresh fruits, and there were a few short readings done. After that, there was a short songfest of some traditional Hebrew songs.

It was beneficial to both the residents and the volunteers. The residents were reunited for an hour and a half with the culture and religion from which they had been separated as a result of being isolated from their community. They also got to visit with families and children, something that was reminiscent of their past years in the community. It often stimulated them to remember and talk about their past experiences—how they celebrated the holidays with their friends and families. They also realized that their people had not forgotten them because they had come to the nursing home to share the holiday.

For the volunteers it was also a very beneficial experience. Because both parents were fully employed during the week, it was very hard for them to make a regular commitment to volunteer weekly, but coming on a monthly basis to share a couple of hours was something they could do. Also, they included their children at a young age so that the children were able to experience the *mitzvah* of *bikur cholim* in a nonthreatening way. Their children were not merely told that one should perform *bikur cholim*, but they were shown it as they shared the experience with their parents. The volunteers learned a lot of history through firsthand stories from the patients. It also was beneficial to some of the volunteers who went with the family, because they were new to *bikur cholim*. They were nervous about visiting alone, but coming in a group helped ease these fears. It did not put pressure on them to have to think about what to say, for there was a planned program. As they grew more comfortable during the course of the visit, they usually found themselves more apt to approach at least one or two patients to talk to individually.

For group visits there is such a variety of activities that could be done. Your imagination is the limit. One rabbi, at a home where I once volunteered, scared away a family that had been visiting monthly to present some kind of Jewish-related program because he told them he needed to screen their presentation in case it duplicated his weekly services. From my experience as a volunteer, I saw this to be a real error because even if there are several presentations on the same theme, there is always a different angle on the presentation; there are new people to meet and connect with; and there are so few acts of *bikur cholim* that at any one moment, there never seems to be a situation in which a resident is harmed by feeling that that there are too many people who care about him.

Some possible group ideas are songfests, dancing performances, bingo games, card and board game socials, and book discussion groups. One of our local high schools sponsors a special prom evening at one of the nearby nursing homes once a year. Even patients in wheelchairs can dance and be in parades as they remain seated in their chairs and rhythmically move whatever parts of their bodies they can. It is an occasion to get dressed up in fancy clothes, and a variety of home-baked foods are brought in for a special buffet supper. Corsages and boutonnieres are given to the patients. This creates an opportunity to involve teenagers in the process of *bikur cholim* in a way that may be easier for them than one-on-one visiting, and it reconnects the elderly to the world of our youth. There are often interesting stories traded all around.

The members of my own synagogue (North Shore Jewish Center in Port Jefferson Station, New York) make a commitment every Christmas to bring flowers to a local hospital, to patients who must be away from their community on a holiday that is important to them. Besides being a gesture of goodwill between Jews and Christians, this also has several other benefits. For the patients, it shows that they are not forgotten and forsaken because they are not a part of the outside community at the moment. For the volunteers, it provides an organized opportunity to perform *bikur cholim*. It also is a chance for parents and children to do this together in a relatively comfortable way.

Still another concept for *bikur cholim* is pet visits. Many patients carry fond memories of their dogs and cats whom they could talk to and from whom they could obtain unconditional love. Being in a nursing home or hospital removes them from the realm of this unconditional love. Many nursing homes have witnessed the value of pet visits. For example, one administrator spoke of a resident named Hannah who lived in the home for five years. Hannah was usually very sullen and rarely spoke more than a few words at a time. Then one day a woman who was coming from visiting her father was outside in the front of the home walking her dog, who had been waiting in the car while the woman visited. Whether it was instinct or something else, the dog approached Hannah's wheelchair and jumped up into Hannah's lap. The owner was embarrassed and started to apologize, but then she looked at Hannah and stopped short. The aide who had brought Hannah outside for a little sun was amazed, too. Hannah sat there calmly clutching the dog and stroking his back. A big smile lit up her face and she began singing a Yiddish song softly to the dog. In order to be permitted to leave, the owner promised to bring her dog to see Hannah on a regular weekly basis, and she has. The nursing home has since adopted a program whereby some pet owners bring their animals to visit once a week. As a matter of fact, pet visiting is one of the jobs they now list on their volunteer applications. Some volunteers have told the director of volunteers that patients' reactions to their pets creates a ready-made topic of conversation. One volunteer had only planned to visit once a month, but the overwhelming positive response by some patients has made her realize the necessity of doing it more frequently; she gets a lot out of the visits, too.

## THE DEPARTURE

Now that I have discussed the content of the visit, what to say, how to say it, and what to do during the visit, next comes the important question of how and when to end it.

If we continue to keep in mind that our aim in *bikur cholim* is to comfort the patient with our presence, we will try to be mindful of not staying too long. Sometimes at the beginning of the visit, after you are granted permission to stay, it is good to say that if the patient gets tired during the visit, he should let you know. Also, during the visit, look for cues from him that indicate fatigue. If he is yawning or dozing, say something like: "You seem to be tired. Would you like me to leave and let you get some rest? Then I could come back another day when you might not be as tired."

By the patient's answer, you'll know what to do. He might reply: "I didn't realize I would be so tired. I guess I'm still weak from my surgery. I appreciate your coming to see me today. I really enjoyed the visit and hope you will come again another day." Or he could say: "I'm really enjoying your visit. It makes me feel relaxed in a way I haven't felt for several days. I'd like you to stay a little while longer, if you don't mind."

From the patient's answer, you should be able to know whether or not he feels your visit is too long and needs to be ended. It is important to say things in such a way that the patient feels comfortable telling you he is not feeling up to the visit. It is also important that you, as a volunteer, do not feel that the visit was a failure because the patient did not allow it to go on for a long time.

Now, what about times when the volunteer feels a need to end the visit? There may be several reasons why you will need to do this. The most common one is that your time is limited and you have other obligations. But another reason to leave may also have to do with your difficulty in handling the visit for one or more of the following reasons: Perhaps the patient's illness is something you find difficult to deal with. Maybe this patient's symptoms remind you of the difficult ordeal you just went through with your mother, who died only six months ago of cancer. You have not got over that and are not able to relive the pain at this time.

There are polite ways to end such a visit before you do something out of control. The uncomfortable volunteer might say something like this: "I'm sorry that it seems like you are in a lot of pain. I hope the pain will be less as time goes on. I just stopped in for a minute to give you my best wishes. I will say a prayer for you. Take care!"

Perhaps the patient has a disease like AIDS, and the volunteer is prejudiced against him because of the lifestyle he led that caused him to contract this disease. If your judgments and prejudices get in the way, then your visit will be too tense for you and will not comfort the patient, because he will sense by your demeanor that you are not listening attentively to his story. Clues about your discomfort will surely come through to the patient by the way you sit and what you say. The longer the visit lasts, the more uncomfortable the host and the guest will become.

Again, before you make a comment that reveals you to be judgmental, find a way to get out of the situation as quickly as possible and without hurting the patient by making prejudiced remarks. You might say something like this: "I'm not able to visit for very long, but I just wanted to stop in to let you know that I send my best wishes for good health."

Perhaps you begin to feel uncomfortable or ill or hungry or need to go to the bathroom. Your mind starts to think about your needs, and you do not pay full attention to the patient. Perhaps it isn't the right time to visit until your needs are alleviated. You might be able to excuse yourself briefly to meet your needs and you could come back afterward, or you might need to go home and come another time. If you can't concentrate on the visit, it is not beneficial to you or to the patient. Too many unsatisfactory visits for a patient might make him turn away from making any effort to welcome volunteers. Why should he bother to host a visit if it is never beneficial to him?

What about the visit that seems to be going along well, when the patient seems to be thriving on your attention and does not seem to want it to end? Try to end it at a natural break. For example, he is talking about his childhood in Brooklyn and then begins to talk about how the family moved to Long Island. You could say: "I have to leave now to pick up my daughter from her swim practice, but I'd like to come back on Thursday at 4:00 to hear more about your Long Island life. I really learned a lot from you about what it was like to live in Brooklyn when it was a Jewish neighborhood." Will it hurt the patient's feelings if you have to end the visit? Perhaps the patient will be disappointed, but he won't be devastated if you tell him why you need to leave—family obligations, and so forth—and talk to him about the positive aspects of this visit (what benefits you received from spending time with him). Thus, you validate him as a good host. You should also offer a time when you will return for another visit. Only offer another visit if you really plan to follow through with it, and try to give a specific day and time when you will return, if possible. Perhaps you might leave a momento of your visit. This could be a card with the name and number of your volunteer agency or the *bikur cholim* society associated with your volunteer work. What you leave for the patient is his connection to the outside world. It is proof to him that someone cares about his well-being. It is his connection to Judaism.

## AFTER THE VISIT

After you leave the patient, do you find that you spend a lot of time thinking about the session? That is a very common reaction. It is important to reflect on the visit because that is how to learn how to become an even better volunteer. You ask yourself some central questions. Did you find the visit healthy or stressful? Do

92

you think the patient benefited? Did you benefit? These are the key questions that should be asked in order for you to continue to grow in your *bikur cholim* experience.

Overinvolvement: It is not unhealthy to think about the patient and perhaps say a silent prayer or a *Mi Shebarach* at the synagogue for the patient's well-being. Perhaps you will talk about your visit as a matter of course, telling a friend or family member about your experience. As long as you accept that by performing *bikur cholim*, you are doing what you can to help the patient feel as comfortable as he possibly can under the circumstances, and as long as you understand that you do not have control over the physical progression of his disease, then *bikur cholim* can be a healthy experience for you.

If you find that you are constantly thinking about the patient, that you are owning the patient as your responsibility, that you feel as if you are responsible for his illness and are frustrated that you cannot cure it, that you are identifying with the patient's age and family background and are beginning to think that you could be in that situation, then you may be overinvolved. This can be harmful to you, as the patient's condition begins to take over your life. You become distracted at home and in your other roles and become unable to perform as usual. It can also harm the patient, especially if these feelings interfere with your allowing the patient to talk freely about his problems and deal with feelings regarding his illness.

For the benefit of both the volunteer and the patient, an overinvolved volunteer may need to take time off from seeing the patient and should consult the director of volunteers or the *bikur cholim* Society coordinator. There may be support groups available to help you deal with this issue. The overinvolved volunteer must be able to come to terms with his reaching the limit of what he is able to handle emotionally. He must step back for a while to understand these stresses; then he can learn new and healthier ways to deal with them. If the overinvolved volunteer still feels an obligation to continue with *bikur cholim*, he can look for a different kind of assignment. For example, perhaps he could work in the hospital's physical therapy program where, instead of doing one-on-one visits, he might transport patients to and from their physical therapy sessions.

## Stress

After a session with a patient, a volunteer might experience some kind of stress. Many new situations tend to produce stress. After one leaves the situation, it is not uncommon to think about what went on and what one could have said to have made the situation better. How often do we think, "If only I had said that instead of what I did say!"

Stress is positive if it serves to help us think about ways to improve, as long as we are not too down on ourselves for what did happen. Stress is a tool for growth if we use it to fine tune our situation so that it becomes better.

Stress is negative when it causes us to focus on what occurred in the worst possible light. If we did such a terrible job the first time, there will be too much pressure on us to make it positive the next time, and besides, a person who cannot find any positives is likely to be totally critical the second time if perfection is not reached. For such a person, stress can become overwhelming and can adversely affect mental and/or physical health.

Every time a volunteer enters a room to perform *bikur cholim*, it is a stressful situation, in that she can never be sure what to expect. Even if the volunteer has known the patient for many months, she enters the room unaware of the changes in the patient's situation since the last visit. If the stress is a cue to the volunteer to do her best to make the visit as beneficial as possible to both the patient and herself, then it is positive.

## Confidentiality

Most volunteer training includes the issue of confidentiality. Usually, the rule is made clear that what goes on in the session between the volunteer and the patient is not permitted to be discussed with others on the outside. The patient has the right to know that what he talks about with his *bikur cholim* visitor is not going to be discussed with his family, with the medical staff, or with any outsiders. There are, of course, a few exceptions: If the patient would like you to tell the nurse about some pain he is experiencing or if there are other issues for which he would like you to advocate for him, then you can if you are able. Let the patient know, in that case, what you will and will not be doing. If the patient tells you he is going to harm himself, then you should let the appropriate authorities (nurses, doctors, etc.) know of his plan.

People who find the courage to volunteer, when so many others find the excuse not to, are well meaning and go into *bikur cholim* with a warm heart. Such an attitude, along with basic instincts and the right match, will make *bikur cholim* work. We all see in retrospect how we could have handled things better. Don't be afraid of doing things wrong. The skills and principles that were discussed in this chapter are meant to be ways to fine tune that basic skill. Then the positive experience of *bikur cholim* will become still more positive as we experience more and more situations and find ourselves able to grow as we progress from one level of *bikur cholim* to another.

In conclusion, here is a brief review of some of the do's and don'ts of *bikur cholim* that were discussed so far.

## A REVIEW OF DO'S AND DON'TS FOR *BIKUR CHOLIM* VOLUNTEERS

### Reasons to Volunteer

DO:

Choose to volunteer because you feel that you can benefit from it.
Choose to volunteer because you can see the importance of helping others who are sick and elderly to experience growth through your visits.

DON'T:

Feel forced to volunteer just because others tell you that you have to.

Be so stressed about volunteering that you are likely to panic and find yourself unable to follow your instincts.

## Selecting the Right Match

DO:

Explore agencies and *bikur cholim* societies to set up and supervise your matches.

Explore the kinds of jobs available for *bikur cholim*.

Take your time in selecting the match that you feel you can handle.

Visit the setting you feel you might be interested in working in.

DON'T:

Select a setting just because a friend tells you to.

Blindly select and commit to a setting just because it is located in your area.

Panic and back out of *bikur cholim* if a particular job profile scares you.

## Preparation for the Visit

DO:

Think positively about the experience of *bikur cholim*.

Dress in comfortable, presentable clothing that you would normally wear if visiting socially with friends, or wear a hospital jacket or uniform if required by the agency.

Try to go at a time when you don't expect many distractions, such as hunger, the need to go to the bathroom, a close deadline to leave to pick up your child from school, and so forth.

Prepare some positive topics to talk about.

Have an open mind.

If you would like to bring a gift, choose something that will help the patient connect to the outside world and to Judaism.

If you are considering visiting an enemy, call ahead of time to assess the patient's feelings about your visit, and visit only if the patient appears to be comfortable with seeing you.

## DON'T:

Visit early in the morning or late at night or right before surgery unless the patient requests it.

Visit patients with digestive disorders, contagious diseases, or illnesses such as a severe headache, when it will disturb the patient or disrupt the quiet that is needed for recovery.

Visit enemies if the purpose of the visit might make the patient feel that you are there to gloat over the illness.

Wear perfume or aftershave, since the patient may be hypersensitive to odors.

Bring bad news to the patient.

Bring any prejudiced opinions.

Bring food unless you know that the patient is not on a restricted diet and is allowed to have it.

### Entering the Room

## DO:

Knock on the door to announce your presence.

Announce who you are and what agency you represent.

Ask permission to enter the room.

Wait, if it appears that there are already several visitors there, or if you can't wait, let the patient know that you'll come back another time.

Leave a note if the patient is asleep or out of the room when you come.

Smile and make a cheerful entrance.

DON'T:

>Insist on visiting if the patient does not want a visitor.
>
>Feel insulted if the patient does not want you to visit at this time.
>
>Enter the room if medical staff persons are in there providing service to the patient.
>
>Enter the room with a frown on your face.

## The Introduction

DO:

>Introduce yourself and explain why you are here.
>
>Act polite and respectful of the patient.
>
>Remember that you are the guest, and the patient is your host.
>
>Address the patient formally until you get to know him better.
>
>Ask permission to sit and/or to do activities that you think might make the patient more comfortable, such as fluffing his pillows.
>
>Ask a general question regarding patient's health.
>
>Prepare yourself to listen actively.

DON'T:

>Just walk in and start talking until you explain who you are.
>
>Take over and start doing things for the patient that you judge would make him comfortable.
>
>Ask a question and start to interrupt the answer with your own thoughts and feelings.
>
>Prepare any false advice or comforting words that will merely be said because it makes you comfortable to say them.

## The Visit

DO:

>Listen to what the patient has to say.

Help the patient by acknowledging the validity of what he has to say.

Help the patient express feelings and thereby allow him to come to terms with the situation.

Accept that the patient may have some anger and know that it is not directed at you personally.

Accept that you have no power to make the illness better or worse but that your being there with the patient may have an effect on his being able to deal with the situation in a more positive way.

Sit facing the patient and look directly at him as he speaks.

Nod your head in agreement and ask questions that encourage the patient to continue with his story, to tell you more.

Bring in objects that help connect the patient to the Jewish community and to his outside world in general.

If you feel comfortable doing so, ask the patient if you can hold his hand.

If you are able to, offer a prayer or a good wish to the patient.

Advocate for the patient by making the staff or family aware of the needs he expresses to you.

Keep in confidence what the patient has revealed to you, unless he wants you to talk to someone about it or unless he expresses doing harm to himself.

End the visit if the situation becomes too stressful or uncomfortable to you.

## DON'T:

Interject your own experiences or feelings regarding what the patient is saying.

Question medical treatment or hospital issues, even if the patient does that in his complaints to you.

Take sides if a patient talks about a dispute with family or staff.

Let your mind wander to your own issues, which may cause you to stop listening.

Become prejudiced toward the patient if his lifestyle and values do not necessarily agree with yours.

Be afraid of silence.

Feel that you are under pressure to find a topic to talk about if there is silence.

Change a topic just because you are uncomfortable dealing with it.

Talk about a patient who seems unable to hear or to understand in that patient's presence.

Sit on the patient's bed unless he asks you to.

Feel an obligation to fix the situation.

## The Departure

DO:

Tell the patient when you first come in that if he starts to feel sleepy or needs to be alone, he should let you know his needs.

Look for clues in the patient's behavior that might indicate that your visit is too long and should end.

Let the patient know ahead of time if you have another commitment and have to leave by a certain time.

Try to find a way to break up the patient's story in an orderly way if you need to leave while he is still in the middle of it.

Tell the patient when you can come back again if you are planning to return.

Leave with a polite excuse if you find your mind wandering or you're being prejudiced and judgmental.

DON'T:

Stay if you are uncomfortable physically and/or mentally and cannot pay full attention to the patient's story.

End the visit abruptly.

Say you will come back for another visit if you don't intend to.

## After the Visit

DO:

Remember the positives from this experience.

Tell others about the importance of doing *bikur cholim.*

Allow any stresses to help you find ways to improve your next *bikur cholim* visit.

Allow yourself to grow in a positive way from each new experience.

Take pride in your work.

DON'T:

Overcriticize yourself for things you now see that could have been improved.

Become so overinvolved with the patient that it interferes with your normal family and personal activities.

The next two chapters deal with the process of recruiting and keeping volunteers. In chapter 7 I discuss how to start a *bikur cholim* group, including such issues as how to recruit agencies and members to volunteer, how to train them with specific exercises, and how to keep volunteers once you have them. Chapter 8 covers the organization of volunteer services from two Jewish nursing homes that appear to have highly successful volunteer programs.

The how-to's of these two chapters are extremely important. An agency can have the most enthusiastic volunteers, but if it is unable to match its volunteer to a satisfying experience, in which the volunteer feels some benefit from the match, it will not be able to keep that volunteer. I know from my own experience that my volunteer time lessened when I found myself going onto my assigned floor to pass out ice water from patient to patient. At first, I saw my job as an icebreaker—a way to enter rooms and have access to seeing patients—but some days I would sense that there wasn't anyone who wanted to talk, and I would go home feeling that I could have used that time to clean my house.

The next two chapters deal with how to make *bikur cholim* an exciting experience for everyone involved. The key to success is to get the volunteer and keep him.

101

# CHAPTER SEVEN

# HOW TO START A *BIKUR CHOLIM* COMMITTEE

A *bikur cholim* committee should be well organized and well planned in order to successfully locate specific volunteer jobs and find volunteers who are capable of performing the specified job duties. It needs members to train volunteers for their jobs, to assist with the match of the volunteer to the job, and to assess the volunteer's job performance. If the job match is poor, then a committee chairperson needs to be available to change the match, to work with the volunteer on further training, and to comfort the volunteer if there are any specific issues or problems.

It would be helpful to select a chairperson who either is a skilled volunteer or who has training in psychology or social work. Some *bikur cholim* committees might have two chairpersons, one who does administrative duties and one who performs clinical duties.

The administrative chairperson has organizational skills and keeps records. He knows job descriptions and who is volunteering at what job and which hours the volunteer has available. He can use this information to make matches, as requests for visitors and services come to him from outside agencies.

The clinical chairperson is in charge of training and support. If visitors have questions or issues to deal with in regard to their *bikur cholim* duties, the clinical chairperson gives support. He also sets up peer support systems and trainings. It is important for volunteers to have ongoing support. Without the support, they may feel too much pressure and may decide to drop out. With support, they are more likely to work through their frustrations and enrich their *bikur cholim* experiences as they tackle the obstacles, or, if the obstacles are too difficult, they could change to a different job that might be more suited to their talents.

This chapter will be specific about how to organize the *bikur cholim* committee and keep it alive: topics such as who can organize it, who will sponsor it, how to select chairpersons, how to assess needs for services, how to recruit members, how to match members to assignments, how to keep members and help them enrich their experiences, and how to publicize to help with ongoing recruitment.

## WHO CAN ORGANIZE A *BIKUR CHOLIM* COMMITTEE?

Many times a rabbi, who is so often overtaxed in his job (part of which is to visit congregants who are ill and to counsel families whose members are sick and hospitalized), may look for ways to provide services more efficiently. By organizing a core of volunteers within the synagogue, the rabbi can free up some of his time and in doing so can help congregants perform a *mitzvah* that may benefit them more than by just creating the feeling that they are performing a good deed. It can help them understand life, appreciate their own health and well-being, and see that there are people available for them if they should someday be in that situation. It can help families who choose to include their children in the *mitzvah* in order to teach them moral values by example. For the patients and their families, the use of *bikur cholim* volunteers, in addition to the rabbi's visits, gives them more services and shows them that the community cares.

104

To organize a *bikur cholim* committee within the synagogue, the rabbi should look for a group within that would agree to run it. In order to find one, the rabbi should go to meetings of various organizations to speak about *bikur cholim* and thereby seek out sponsors. A good candidate for the formation of a committee would be a Sisterhood or a men's club, or perhaps both doing it jointly.

A synagogue usually covers a small area and the patients who are visited, at least at first, would be congregation members. What about others who need *bikur cholim* visitors? There are also other agencies and groups that might be able to sponsor more broad-based *bikur cholim* committees, and I will mention some of these, too.

A Jewish community center, which often houses meetings from various groups in the area, might have some groups that would be interested in organizing a *bikur cholim* committee. One example might be a senior citizen's program meeting in that location. Members could live in all different areas of the community, and they may really see a need since they are at an age when illness is more likely to strike them and when some of the people who need the services may be their own friends or acquaintances.

Other sources to help organize a committee could be nonprofit organizations such as Hadassah or ORT (Organization for Rehabilitation Through Training). Although they do a lot of fundraising for their causes, some of their main precepts are good health care, in the case of Hadassah, and helping each person become independent by teaching work skills, for ORT. By administering to the sick and elderly, both organizations can help promote and enhance their principles.

Service organizations like Jewish Family Service agencies and those local agencies that serve the aged often encounter people who need *bikur cholim* services. They may agree to administer a *bikur cholim* committee so that they can match volunteers to their needs.

Independent organizations could be formed to run a *bikur cholim* committee, if, for example, there is a group of concerned citizens that sees a need for this service.

A Jewish Communal Planning Council also may be the agency to organize a *bikur cholim* committee. In 1994 I chaired a committee through the Suffolk (New York) Jewish Communal Planning Council, in which we first did a study to assess the number of synagogues in the county who had *bikur cholim* programs, who did not have them, and who wanted additional training programs to possibly form or strengthen their programs. Then we also polled nursing and adult homes in regard to their needs for Jewish volunteers. Finally, we held a *bikur cholim* training given by Rabbi Isaac Trainin and his staff from the Coordinating Council on Bikur Cholim. I will give further details and will reproduce the specific questionnaires in the section on assessing needs for services.

## WHO CAN SPONSOR A *BIKUR CHOLIM* COMMITTEE?

You might say that if a *bikur cholim* committee is made up of volunteers, then there should be no expenses and thus no need for anyone to sponsor or fund such a committee.

The truth is that there are, in fact, certain expenses and some considerations why it would be most beneficial to have a sponsor. Some expenses include: (1) Mailings and phone calls to assess specific needs—I am going to suggest that this should be done prior to starting a *bikur cholim* program. Otherwise, there may be too much inefficiency when no one really knows what the needs are and, in fact, whether a need for *bikur cholim* even exists; (2) Newspaper ads to try to interest volunteers. Many of the ads could be free if they are sent in as community service ads, but a paid ad is guaranteed to be in a particular edition, whereas a community service ad only appears if space is available; (3) Mailings and phone calls to procure potential members; (4) Forms for volunteers to fill out; and (5) Funds to rent a space to hold committee meetings (if the group cannot get an agency to donate space free of charge).

If an agency sponsors the *bikur cholim* committee, it can be very beneficial. The agency can provide a meeting room and also may publicize the program in its mailings and statement of services provided. If the *bikur cholim* committee seeks referrals for its services, it is more likely to receive cooperation if it can identify itself as being connected with a specific agency. The agency itself may need the service for its clients.

As part of the agency's budget, some of the expenses of the *bikur cholim* committee may be covered.

A *bikur cholim* committee may also look to a federation to obtain a funding grant.

## SELECTING A CHAIRPERSON FOR THE COMMITTEE

At this point the chairperson should be someone who will understand the logic of organization and what needs to be done in a step-by-step process of setting up a program. He should be someone who will set up a method to research the areas of need for the volunteers.

The chairperson can delegate the responsibilities to the committee members so that each member takes part in completing the research (or he can do the research by himself). He should give a tentative time frame for the research to be concluded and then should set up a next meeting date to bring together research findings.

Without this research the program might be set up, but it could be very inefficient if there is no specific list of needs, and volunteers will have no sense of organization. A chaotic program has more of a chance to fail because confusion does not allow the volunteer to feel a sense of pride for work well done when he does not really even know what he is supposed to do. Such a volunteer is much more likely to quit.

The person who volunteers or is asked to be chairperson has to understand the importance of these job duties and needs to agree to do them.

After the research for needs is completed and a tentative list of organization is made up, some *bikkur cholim* committees may then select an additional *bikkur cholim* chairperson to take on clinical direction-trainings, work on job satisfaction, support for volunteers, and so forth. The administrative chairperson should also remain to keep things running smoothly by keeping a continuous list of needs as they are called in by an agency and by matching volunteers to these needs.

## ASSESSING NEEDS FOR *BIKUR CHOLIM* SERVICES

How does the chairperson know where to place volunteers or how many volunteers are needed? How does the chairperson know what types of skills are needed from the volunteers? These are the key questions that must be answered before an effective *bikur cholim* society can be created.

As a volunteer for the Suffolk Jewish Communal Planning Council, I chaired a committee that spent approximately six months trying to answer these questions so that we could learn whether or not it would be feasible to offer *bikur cholim* training to interested groups in Suffolk County.

The task began with a mailing to all the synagogues in the county. Here is a copy of the questionnaire that we sent, so you can get an idea of what you might want to do. The letter was written on letterhead stationery to show that there was an established agency involved, and that gave the survey some credibility. We also began the letter with a statement about the organization, to help responders know who they were giving their replies to.

Dear Friend:

The Suffolk Jewish Communal Planning Council, an umbrella organization of representative leaders of the Suffolk Jewish community, is establishing a program to coordinate and expand *bikur cholim* (visiting the sick) programs currently existing in our area. Our first step is to take a survey of those current programs. You can help us in our efforts by taking a few moments to answer the questions below. (If you need more space, please use the back of the form or additional sheets.)

We would like to complete our survey by June 1st and have enclosed a self-addressed envelope for your convenience. Thank you for your cooperation.

Sincerely,
Sharon S. Epstein
Coordinator, Bikur Cholim Training Program

Name of Organization
Contact Person
Phone Number

1. Does your synagogue or organization currently have a *bikur cholim* program?

If so, please provide us with a description of the program. We are interested in such questions as which hospitals and other institutions are visited? How often do these visits occur? How many people are involved in the program?

2. If you don't currently have a *bikur cholim* program, would you be interested in learning about how to establish one, including how volunteers can receive training?

Follow-up calls were made to synagogues and organizations that did not return the questionnaires.

The following information was obtained through this portion of the survey: Eighteen of the twenty-eight synagogues that were contacted indicated that they had no formal program, although the rabbi often visited members of the synagogue who were ill. Two very small congregations indicated that they visit their own members but are too small to want to establish any ongoing *bikur cholim* programs. One synagogue located in a resort area indicated that most congregants are just summer and weekend residents and so would be unable to establish an ongoing *bikur cholim* program. Twenty synagogues indicated an interest in obtaining more information on *bikur cholim* training. These included some that already had formal programs but would like to expand these programs.

The next step in the research process included a second survey, this time to ascertain the need for volunteers. The following is a copy of the letter that was sent to all adult and nursing homes in Suffolk County:

Dear Friend:

The Suffolk Jewish Communal Planning Council, an umbrella organization of representative leaders of the Suffolk Jewish community, is establishing a program to coordinate and expand the *bikur cholim* (visiting the sick) programs currently existing in our area.

Our first step is to take a survey of those current programs. You can help us in our efforts by taking a few moments to answer the questions below. (If you need more space, please use the back or additional sheets.)

We would like to complete our survey by mid-August and have enclosed a self-addressed envelope for your convenience. Thank you for your cooperation.

Sincerely,
Sharon S. Epstein
Coordinator, Bikur Cholim Training Program

Name of Organization
Contact Person
Phone Number

1. Does your facility have any Jewish patients (residents)?_____
Approximately how many?_____

2. Do you have any volunteers from synagogues or Jewish organizations who come to visit patients on a regular basis (a daily or weekly visit, monthly, at holiday time only, etc.)?

3a. Does your agency have an existing program to train volunteers who wish to become involved in regular visiting or activities with your residents?_____

b. Do you feel that your Jewish patients might benefit if we were able to organize and train Jewish people in the community to visit them on a regular basis?_____

4. Do you have any questions, concerns, or comments about our desire to set up and train volunteers to visit Jewish patients at your agency?

Phone calls were made to follow up on some of the surveys that were not returned.

The results of this survey were as follows: Of the twenty-nine nursing homes who completed the survey, only one indicated that it had only two Jewish patients and felt that these patients would not benefit from Jewish volunteers. Most of the rest, including other homes with only one or two Jewish residents, were enthusiastic about having Jewish volunteers either specifically to present a program for Jewish holidays and/or to be visitors on a regular and more frequent basis. Some homes in one specific area of the county indicated that for the High Holidays, a synagogue in the area drops off a tape of the holiday service for Jewish residents to view. One home indicated that the recreation program director, who was not Jewish, often read material about various Jewish holidays and would present a program based on her research to her Jewish residents. The consensus, even at homes where there were only a few Jewish residents, was that establishing a connection for a Jewish patient to the Jewish culture and to the Jewish community itself was very beneficial.

Some adult homes responded to the survey, and others were phoned. It was discovered that in the case of adult homes, many residents were able to get around on their own during the day and did not really experience that separation from the community that nursing patients had. Therefore, the need for *bikur cholim* volunteers in such a setting was not so urgent.

Conclusions from the two surveys presented in this assessment indicated a potential source of *bikur cholim* volunteers with the synagogues as the sponsoring agencies and the need for the volunteers at a variety of nursing homes located throughout Suffolk County. Since we found a source of potential volunteers and a need for the service, we were then able to proceed with an organized training and potential matches.

The next step in the procedure was to hold a seminar and training to which we could invite potential volunteers as well as representatives from nursing homes and hospitals that might have the need for *bikur cholim* volunteers.

A letter was sent to Rabbi Isaac Trainin, executive vice-president of the Coordinating Council on Bikur Cholim, to request his presence and expertise on training volunteers. The letter read as follows:

Dear Rabbi Trainin:

The Suffolk Jewish Communal Planning Council would like to invite you to be a guest speaker at a training program for people to become involved with *bikur cholim*. The program will be held on Sunday, April _____ from _____ to _____.

As a preparation to this training program, the council did a survey of the synagogues and adult and nursing homes in Suffolk County to assess the need for *bikur cholim* programs. Many synagogues had no formal programs for *bikur cholim* but were interested in getting more information on establishing such programs. Adult and nursing home personnel expressed the need for Jewish volunteers.

We paired synagogues in which the desire to establish *bikur cholim* programs was expressed with homes in their geographical areas that expressed the need for Jewish volunteers. We plan to send these lists to the synagogues, along with an invitation to come to this program. The program will provide preparation to volunteers before they actually visit the adult and nursing homes in their area.

Since you have experience doing *bikur cholim* training, we would like to ask for your assistance in planning and presenting this seminar. In particular, we think program participants will be enriched by a discussion of your experiences. We expect a mixed audience of both teens and adults. We think such material as anecdotes about the value of *bikur cholim*, its role in Jewish history, and your involvement would be interesting. We especially need guidance in how to train these potential volunteers. We would welcome written materials, suggestions for visiting, how to deal with potential problems, how to talk to patients and the elderly, and other information you think is pertinent in training a volunteer. We think that participants would enjoy the opportunity for a question and answer period.

We envision two parts to the program. First, you will make a presentation. We will then divide into two groups, adult and teen volunteers, giving each any special training they might need. Local experts will guide these groups.

We certainly hope you will be able to be with us for this important event.

Thank you very much.
Sincerely,
Susan Lustig
Executive Director

# RECRUITING MEMBERS FOR THE *BIKUR CHOLIM* PROGRAM

Now that the research has clearly established the need for *bikur cholim* and some of the particular places that have the need, the next step in the *bikur cholim* process is to recruit potential members.

At the Suffolk Jewish Communal Planning Council we decided to start by offering a training to interested members of the community. By doing this, we were able to pass out information on what the process is like and where it could be done. It was a fact-finding seminar to help potential volunteers feel comfortable, first in understanding the process and then in gradually easing themselves into actually performing the task. It was also helpful to agencies that wanted to obtain *bikur cholim* volunteers. They sent members from their staff to talk about their specific needs and to try to recruit volunteers, which I will address in further detail later in the section on "Making A Match."

The key to making this seminar work is to advertise the time, place, and topic so that interested people can attend. First we wrote letters to the Jewish community through the use of the synagogue and some of its groups. Following is a sample of the letter we sent. We mailed it as early as possible in order to give interested rabbis a chance to advertise it from the pulpit and to allow synagogue bulletins a chance to put it in their calendar of events.

Dear (Rabbi, Synagogue President, Sisterhood, Brotherhood, Youth Leader),

I am writing this letter on behalf of the Suffolk Jewish Communal Planning Council. In June we surveyed all the synagogues in Suffolk County to ask about programs they might have for visiting the sick, *bikur cholim*. We also inquired about whether those who had such programs would be interested in expanding them and whether those without such programs would be interested in getting training information to begin such programs.

We also surveyed adult and nursing homes in Suffolk County to find out whether they had a Jewish population, and if so, whether they had volunteers who came to visit at holiday times and as regular visitors.

We discovered that many synagogues did not have formal *bikur cholim* programs but indicated an interest in learning more about establishing such programs. Many synagogues with programs indicated an interest in expanding such programs.

Adult and nursing homes in general indicated a need for Jewish visitors. Even homes with a very small Jewish population felt it would be beneficial to provide Jewish visitors for their Jewish residents. Visiting can be done in groups to present holiday materials for those who are not comfortable visiting alone, or it could be done individually.

We have enclosed a list of synagogues with nursing homes in your geographical area that have expressed a desire for Jewish visitors.

We would like to extend our invitation to you to send representatives to our *bikur cholim* training and information workshop to be held on _____ at the Suffolk Y on 74 Hauppauge Road, Commack, NY 11725.

We would also like to encourage teenagers from youth groups to become involved.

Please let us know how many will attend. If you have any questions, please call the Suffolk Jewish Communal Planning Council at 462-5826.

Sincerely,
Sharon S. Epstein
Coordinator, Bikur Cholim Training program

114

Besides sending mailings to what is perceived as the target population, one should also advertise in the newspapers and on local radio and TV stations that publish community service ads free of charge. If there is a source of money available, one might want to put in some creative paid ads and also print up fliers to advertise the event. Fliers can be placed in synagogues, libraries, storefronts, and wherever else you think potentially interested people might go. Just remember to ask permission before you leave your flier. If the place deems it of community interest and not offensive, permission will usually be granted to have it displayed.

In regard to press releases for free ads, one should generally send them in to newspapers and radio and TV stations three weeks to one month ahead of time. They use news releases only as space permits. Select local Jewish newspapers as well as community papers. The principle of a news release is to give a synopsis of your event and let the community know it is happening, with the date, time, and place, and a contact person and number to call if further information is needed. Following is an example of a news release:

News Release
For Immediate Release

For Further Information, Contact:
Susan Lustig, Executive Director
Suffolk Jewish Communal Planning Council
74 Hauppauge Road, Room 53
Commack, NY 11725
(516) 462-5826
Suffolk Jewish Communal Planning Council to Present Training
    on Visiting the Sick

On Sunday April 23, 1995, the Suffolk Jewish Communal Planning Council will sponsor a seminar on *bikur cholim* (visiting the sick and elderly). It will be held from 9:30 A.M.–12:30 P.M. at the Suffolk Y Jewish Community Center, 74 Hauppauge Road, Commack. Adults and teens are welcome, and it is free of charge.

For further information call the council at 462-5826.

This very brief type of news release gives just the basics and usually gets printed by papers in their community calendar of events for the upcoming week. It is a summary for readers of what events are upcoming.

This was printed in one local newspaper, based on our press release:

times_____ and dates

SUNDAY/23
TRAINING SEMINAR FOR VISITING THE SICK

The Suffolk Jewish Communal Planning Council invites interested volunteers to attend an information and training seminar for visiting the sick, to be held from 9:30 A.M.–12:30 P.M. at the Suffolk Y Jewish Community Center, 74 Hauppauge Road, Commack. Call 462-5826.

It is, of course, possible to write much longer news releases. In general, if at all possible, keep the release to one page. Put the most important information at the beginning so that the structure of the release looks like an inverted pyramid, with the crucial information at the beginning. This is important in case papers must cut the release. The characteristic method of doing that cutting is simply to remove the material at the end of the release.

In regard to paid ads and fliers, there are some different principles that come into play. Whereas the aim of the free news release was simply to announce an event to the community so that those already interested in the topic will know about its occurrence, the aim of the paid ad and the flier is twofold. They announce the event, and they also try to persuade or sell the readers on the importance of their participation.

The most basic rule for writing an effective ad is that the organization or group placing the ad focuses on the benefits a potential consumer will obtain from attending a program or volunteering. Don't, that is, list the contents of the program. Instead, list what a person will get for attending. For example, an ad might include the following:

—Learn how to help the ill
—Develop skills in dealing with the elderly

List other benefits you can think of that are important. After the benefits, list the details of where and when the program will take place.

I would like to suggest still another way to recruit members through use of the media. This involves contacting newspapers about your topic. You can make phone calls to the editors to ask them about featuring a story on *bikur cholim*. You can also write a brief article on the topic or a letter to the editor about the importance of *bikur cholim*. Do some research on the topic and present statistics about the elderly population. Possible topics include how people are living longer and how families are scattered, so that children who in the past might have had their elderly parents live with them now have them placed in nursing homes that are often lacking any considerable contact with the Jewish community. Use these statistics to present the urgent need for *bikur cholim*. Contact Jewish papers, synagogue bulletins, and Jewish organization bulletin chair people. Your *bikur cholim* training and program may be of much interest to their constituents, and you can do them a service by providing information for them.

You can also solicit members by speaking at synagogues and at organizational meetings. Our youth is another important area to tap into. Especially in adult and nursing homes, many residents enjoy having programs and visits from youths, and the elderly have many interesting stories that could teach our young people about their past history and culture firsthand. Teaching community service to our youth will get them comfortable with *bikur cholim* before their responsibilities in life allow them to make excuses as to why they can't perform *bikur cholim*.

That again means you need to know research statistics and have interesting anecdotes to present that will show people why *bikur cholim* will benefit them.

Once you have recruited members for your *bikur cholim* committee, how do you help them with placement? Your aim is to find a positive and satisfying match. You want your placement to provide growth and satisfaction to the volunteer and to meet the needs of the organization in need and its patients or residents. Making the match is a very detailed process. This will be discussed in the next section.

## MAKING A MATCH

The *bikur cholim* chairperson must be very organized. This person should be in constant contact with agencies that need volunteers. For example, if the referral is done through the synagogue, the rabbi may pass on a list of congregants who are hospitalized or who are homebound and have a need for *bikur cholim* services. Sometimes congregants may have elderly parents who live with them and who cannot be left alone. If they could find a volunteer to come to their home to supervise their parent for a few hours, it might give the congregants a respite from their duties and allow them a little time for themselves. The rabbi could speak from the pulpit about some of these services the *bikur cholim* volunteer might offer. And in the synagogue bulletin an article could be written, stating that a *bikur cholim* committee exists within the synagogue and that the family of any congregant needing services should contact the rabbi or the *bikur cholim* chairperson.

The *bikur cholim* chairperson also needs to meet with each potential volunteer in person. It would be most helpful to have each volunteer fill out an information sheet so that the chairperson has certain basic facts on file. The volunteer is applying for a job, and it is very important that he explain his skills and talents, the kind of work he feels he can do, and the amount of time and the specific days and hours he is available.

The following is an example of a form that the committee chairperson might ask the volunteer to fill out when they first meet. Of course, your committee might have other questions to add. The advantage of filling out this application is that it gives a synopsis of who the volunteer is and what his skills are. It also provides a basis for asking further questions to help get to know this particular volunteer and hence to help assess whether a match is appropriate.

Bikur Cholim Application

Name: _____

Address: _____

Phone Number: Daytime _____ Evening _____

Occupation: _____

Skills and Talents: _____

_____

Availability to Visit:

_____Daily_____ Twice a Week_____ Weekly_____Twice a Month_____Monthly_____Other (specify)

Days Available_____Hours Available_____

Would Services Be Provided:

_____Individually_____In a Group_____With a Buddy

Kinds of Services I Am Interested in Performing:

Visiting:

_____ people who are in the hospital

_____ people who are homebound

_____ people who reside in nursing or adult homes

_____ people who are terminally ill

_____ people who are mentally ill

Kinds of People I Prefer to Visit:

_____ adults

_____ elderly

_____ children

_____ infants

Kinds of Services I Would Provide

_____ friendly phone calls_____how often?

_____ prepare and deliver a meal_____how often?

_____ food shopping and/or run errands_____how often?

_____ transport to medical appointments

_____ transport and spend a day out___how often?

_____ write letters, organize bills, and so forth

_____ read or share a cassette or video
_____ provide child care_____ number of hours/week
_____ provide holiday programs_____how often?

Kinds of Visits That May Be Difficult for Me to Perform:
_____to terminally patients
_____to people with AIDS
_____to mentally ill people
_____other

Reasons That a Certain Kind of Population Might Be Difficult for Me at This Time_____

_____

Expectations of What the Benefits of *Bikur Cholim* Will Be for Me

_____

_____

The *bikur cholim* chairperson can then talk to the volunteer to clarify some of the answers expressed on this form and to ask the volunteer more about his concerns and questions about the job of volunteering. Besides reading about a person on paper, the chairperson learns from the personal interview other factors that can affect a *bikur cholim* visit. For example, a volunteer might be very nervous and might not look at the *bikur cholim* chairperson during the interview, or the volunteer might not have good listening skills. Such characteristics that are picked up during an initial interview might cue the chairperson into helping the volunteer start off at a level of *bikur cholim* that might be more comfortable than plunging into a one-on-one visit. For example, for his first visit the volunteer might go with a group from the synagogue that is presenting a holiday program at a nursing home. The volunteer can be helpful in transporting patients to the room where the program is to be held and in passing out snacks to patients. He does not have to experience the tension that a one-on-one session might cause. The volunteer can then gradually be eased into eventually having that one-on-one relationship. Part of the *bikur cholim* program will be to provide training and support for volunteers to help them improve their skills and feel more confident. But before this occurs, the volunteer will still be involved at a level that is considered to be comfortable to him at this time.

The chairperson needs to realize that anyone who expresses the desire to perform *bikur cholim* must be directed at once to a level that is comfortable so that this volunteer is not lost, as he might be if he is made to wait too long to perform.

Another task of the *bikur cholim* chairperson is to talk about certain rules for this job. One in particular is confidentiality. A volunteer must not divulge the name and details about the person who is being visited. The patient talks about his situation to his visitor as he would to a friend. A friend is someone you can trust. A friend is someone who will not hurt you. A friend is someone who will listen and will not judge. The visitor can talk about his feelings regarding the visit and about his frustrations and/or positive feelings, but if he gives the specific name and details he is betraying the confidence of a friend.

Another important issue is that *bikur cholim* is a job, and it is an important job. If a volunteer takes it on, he should attempt to perform it to the best of his ability. This includes putting in the hours he has committed to, coming when he says he will come, and not being consistently late.

The data on a form like our previous example provides the basis for the *bikur cholim* interview; having access to that data allows the *bikur cholim* chairperson to organize potential volunteers for each request as it is called in. The chairperson might make a computer program listing certain criteria, such as days, hours, and the nature of the visit, and could enter this volunteer's name under each category that is appropriate. When the need for a volunteer is called in, the chairperson should screen the program very carefully as to the setting and the general nature of the physical and mental health of the patient (Is the patient terminally ill and hooked up to a lot of tubes and other medical equipment? Is the patient mentally ill and prone to uncontrollable outbursts?), the nature of the services that a volunteer could perform, and so forth. This is how the chairperson can hope to find the best match.

After each experience with *bikur cholim*, it would be helpful to both the volunteer and the *bikur cholim* chairperson if a form could be filled out, giving a brief synopsis of the visit and some pertinent details and/or concerns. Recording each visit is good for a couple of reasons: It provides a record of what was accomplished so that if the *bikur cholim* committee needs statistics and data to justify advertising for new members, there is written data available. It also helps in terms of the supervision of, and increased growth for, the volunteer, because it helps him pick out positive and negative aspects of the process of visiting. If he has proper supervision and support, this can help him perfect his skills. It can also help the patient by delineating some of his needs, which might better be provided for if they are made known. The following is an example of a form, just to give you an idea of some of the data you might want to gather. It should be brief because too much paper work often detracts from efficiency of the job.

Bikur Cholim Visitor's Form

Name:_____

Name of person visited:_____

Date of visit:_____

Place visited:_____

Length of visit:_____

Brief summary of the visit:_____

_____

Any special concerns regarding issues discussed or observed during the visit?_____

_____

Any plans for a follow-up visit? If so, specify time and date!

Return this form to the *bikur cholim* chairperson. If there are any immediate concerns, please call the clinical chairperson _____at_____.

Making an educated match is the first job for the *bikur cholim* committee, but the second major task is to keep volunteers inter-

122

ested in continuing as an active part of *bikur cholim* by giving them continued support as they perform their job and by helping them to grow in the job. The next section will discuss how to keep members actively involved. For this, a second *bikur cholim* chairperson might be necessary. This person should have clinical skills and could facilitate support groups and run trainings.

## KEEPING BIKUR CHOLIM MEMBERS INVOLVED

At first, many people offer to try *bikur cholim* because they know it to be a *mitzvah* and because it is a requirement that all Jews be responsible for their fellow Jews. But the excitement and enthusiasm only lasts for so long if the *bikur cholim* volunteer does not feel support from others. The *bikur cholim* volunteer needs to talk about the visits, assess the positives, and learn how to change some of the negatives. Because the visit often occurs in isolation from other volunteers, it is hard to get input from others on how to take credit for the positives and how to improve skills. Monthly group meetings with a clinical committee chairperson and other volunteers could be beneficial in recharging the volunteer. Also, an adviser should be available right away for a volunteer who expresses an immediate concern following a visit. This could be a clinical chairperson or a person who is paired with the volunteer in a buddy system—each to give support to the other as needed, or perhaps a more experienced volunteer who is paired with a new volunteer.

The purpose of the support meeting is to give recognition for work well done, as well as to help sharpen skills and teach new ones.

A person who continues to do the same job all the time sometimes allows it to become a habit. A habit is something that one just does automatically, without thinking. After the first few times, the joy of a new experience fades because there is no room for change and excitement in something that is done automatically. As the excitement fades, one tends to find excuses for not keeping volunteer dates, and eventually one no longer performs these duties. The dinner held once a year to recognize volunteers for their work is soon not enough enticement for them to continue volunteering. A job that has become a habit fails to allow the volunteer to grow in skills, and he never advances to new and exciting work.

Besides support, there might also be monthly trainings to help teach volunteers the skills to improve *bikur cholim* and to go on to more advanced forms of *bikur cholim*.

In this section I will give some examples of specific training sessions that could be held and kinds of issues that could be dealt with to teach positive *bikur cholim* skills. Because each volunteer comes with a certain upbringing, certain values, certain ways of dealing with stress and tensions, and certain prejudices, it is important for the volunteer to participate in trainings to help him recognize these issues and to learn how to deal with them in a positive way. This will benefit the volunteer by helping him grow and will benefit the patient by allowing for more positive interactions.

This training can be presented or facilitated by the clinical *bikur cholim* chairperson, who may be a psychologist or social worker, or the chairperson could ask experienced volunteers or outside experts from the community. The training could include educational lectures on certain pertinent issues, but it is most beneficial if the volunteers are asked to be directly involved in at least part of the session. Role playing, writing, reading, and reflecting are usually of most benefit to the volunteer.

Here are some sample training sessions on a variety of areas of *bikur cholim*:

## WHY DO WE VISIT THE SICK AND ELDERLY?

The facilitator might begin by talking about her own experience with *bikur cholim*, perhaps starting with initial fears about going for the first time, why she chose to go in spite of these fears, what happened during the visit, and her thoughts and feelings after the visit. The facilitator is the role model. She is saying to participants that it is a new experience and that anyone participating in a new experience usually has some fears and worries. Sometimes one starts out with the thought "I visit because it is a *mitzvah* and therefore something I should do." But oftentimes after the visit, one begins to change that thought to "I visit because I gain a lot from the visit. *Bikur cholim* helps me appreciate the preciousness of life. It helps me learn firsthand about my parents' and grandparents' generations, and so forth."

After presenting her anecdotal introduction, the facilitator might go around and ask each participant to share reasons for their involvement, as well as their fears and expectations. These could then be written down on a blackboard or chart paper so that participants could visualize the variety of reasons for performing *bikur cholim* and the kinds of fears and expectations that arise. It helps people to know that *bikur cholim* is a process with skills that can be improved and refined.

Another issue to talk about under this heading is what can one accomplish by performing *bikur cholim*? If a visitor has expectations of doing things he can't do, then if he continues to fail at accomplishing those things, he will become more and more frustrated with the process. He may then give up and not even accomplish what he is capable of accomplishing.

The facilitator may present the following scenario and ask a participant to role play with her:

Yesterday your doctor came into your room and gave you the results of the tests he had been performing. It looks like you have a large tumor on your breast that is growing at a fast rate. The doctor gave you a couple of choices for possible treatment, but you didn't really listen. The only thing that went through your mind at the moment was that you have breast cancer, and all you could think about is how your mother and two aunts died of the disease, and you are scared.

The facilitator visits and introduces herself as a volunteer from your synagogue and asks you how you are feeling.

Pretending to be the patient, the participant starts to talk about her diagnosis. The facilitator jumps in right away to try to comfort her by reassuring her that maybe she will be all right. There has been so much progress in medicine in the last five to ten years that what was considered fatal in the past can often be successfully treated.

The patient replies quickly that maybe that was true, and she stops talking about her feelings about the diagnosis and goes on to another topic.

When the facilitator asks the participant why she stopped talking about what was very obviously bothering her, she replies that the volunteer seemed too uncomfortable to listen and too eager to comfort her with what she could see had no real factual basis. She felt uncomfortable complaining anymore so changed the topic to be more cordial to her visitor.

When the group discussed this issue, they came to the conclusion that a *bikur cholim* volunteer who tries to fix the situation is not really providing a service to the patient.

The same situation was replayed, but this time the facilitator did something different. Instead of saying something reassuring, she tried to encourage the patient to continue to talk through the whole situation—what the doctor had told her about the diagnosis, what her thoughts and feelings were about her current situation. At the end of the session, the patient stated that it was good to have somebody listen as she expressed feelings. Her own children had come to visit yesterday, but she couldn't tell them her feelings. It might scare them to think of the possibility that she might not have long to live.

From these two role plays, participants were asked to write down lists of what an effective volunteer could do and what she could not accomplish. A formal list was written up and handed out.

The can'ts included such issues as making the medical prognosis change, fixing the situation, and changing the person's feelings toward the diagnosis. The can's included providing comfort by being there to listen, bringing in a sense of community and caring, bringing in a sense of Judaism and spirituality, and allowing the patient to become more calm and to sort out her feelings.

## HOW DOES IT FEEL TO BE SICK AND HANDICAPPED?

Sometimes a volunteer is not conscious of some of the limitations a patient's illness presents. In this kind of training, to make the volunteer more aware of some of these handicaps and how to best deal with them, the facilitator will help the volunteer think and feel some of these handicaps. The facilitator might start out with one or two anecdotes, illustrating situations in which there was a misunderstanding between patient and volunteer because the patient could not hear what the volunteer was saying or could not see the volunteer well enough to comprehend what was being said and did not make the volunteer aware of it.

The facilitator might ask participants to tell any stories they have about situations in which there were misunderstandings and if and how they got remedied. Then, potential sources of communication errors could be written on a chart.

The next part of the training involves feeling some of these distractions and trying to communicate to a volunteer in spite of these handicaps. For example, if a wheelchair is available, a volunteer could sit in one of these and speak to a volunteer who stands and then one who sits in a chair at the same level as the wheelchair, and so forth. Assess the effectiveness of communication from different positions. A volunteer patient could put on dark glasses in a dark setting or could wear a pair of glasses that have streaks of paint on them so that his view is distorted and cloudy, as it might be with someone who has a cataract or failing eyesight. One could stuff cotton into one's ears so that one's hearing is impaired. Does the volunteer who is in the handicapped role have any suggestions as to what the other volunteer might do to minimize the handicap? If the "handicapped" volunteer is too proud to mention his difficulty to the volunteer, does the volunteer have any suggestions for the patient to help the situation? Can such suggestions be made to the patient in a polite way so as not to embarrass the patient?

By experiencing the discomfort firsthand, it often helps the volunteer to feel a little more sensitive and understanding of the situation. There may not be a lot that can be done to remedy the situation, but understanding and patience sometimes are enough to make it more comfortable for both the volunteer and the patient.

## THE VISIT—HOW DO WE LISTEN EFFECTIVELY?

The facilitator can start with an anecdote about worrying what to say before making a *bikur cholim* visit and can then talk about how the visit worked out so that his worry was actually in vain.

Then participants might talk about their own experiences when they were anxiously anticipating a visit to a friend, a relative, perhaps a child's teacher, and so forth, and how the visit turned out differently than expected.

The facilitator can then ask participants to write down what they do to show that they are listening, what interferences might distract them from listening, and what they gain from listening. These experiences can then be shared and listed on a chart.

Finally, there should be some role playing. The facilitator can give a specific situation to be played out by a "patient" and a volunteer in which the volunteer will try to give full attention to what the patient is saying. At the end, other members should give feedback regarding what was done to show effective listening and what distracted from effective listening. The "patient" and the volunteer should also talk about their feelings in the process. What did they gain from *bikur cholim*?

Another role play should be done, but this time the volunteer would be instructed by the facilitator that after a certain cue, he should try to find whatever ways he can to become distracted and try not to effectively listen to the patient as he had done in the beginning. At the end of this role play, members will give feedback on effective listening. The "patient" and the volunteer should also discuss their feelings regarding this process.

Conclude with do's and don'ts of effective listening that are generated by participants.

## DO OUR OWN JUDGMENTS AND VALUES AFFECT OUR *BIKUR CHOLIM* SKILLS?

We are all raised in families and cultures in which we are taught certain values. Sometimes we may meet people from different cultures or from different lifestyles who do not seem to act on the same values that we have. Does our judgment get in the way and affect our listening skills when we go to visit such a person who is hospitalized and ill?

An exercise that might help participants recognize their attitudes and how they affect the performance of *bikur cholim* might start by examining oneself and one's changes in flexibility in coping as one matures.

For example, I only remember a few select episodes that occurred when I was a young child. One seemingly insignificant incident that occurred when I was five years old particularly comes to mind. I had been playing with my friend who lived next door, and her family had bought some Trix cereal, which had just newly been marketed. My friend's mother allowed us to snack on the cereal, and we liked it because it was one of many sweetened cereals that would soon hit the cereal market. A couple of days later while we sat on our front porch, a woman came by, professing to be from a marketing company and looking for children to try a new cereal called Trix. She asked me if I had ever tasted this cereal before, and I lied and said, "no." Then she asked my mother if I was allowed to try it, and when the answer was in the affirmative, she offered me a sample and asked me a few questions on the survey she was doing.

I was taught not to lie and am not sure why I did lie. That was a seemingly harmless lie, but because, as a child, I was taught by my family that it is wrong to lie, then it was clear to me at age five that I did something wrong. I'm sure that this incident sticks out in my mind because at that age, any lie was a serious breach of family ethics. Coincidentally, I have no memory of my first day of kindergarten, which also occurred around that time.

With maturity, I have, of course, fine-tuned my skills. While I basically believe that one should not lie, there are cases in which I do lie—for example, to prevent myself from hurting another person's feelings.

As one matures, one learns to fine-tune beliefs and skills to fit the situation. One allows oneself to become flexible and learns not to be judgmental if there is a valid reason for the action one has taken.

In this session, the facilitator might start with an anecdote similar to the one just given to show how we fine-tune basic skills as we mature. Then there may be several written scenarios to give to participants and ask them to respond to. Here are some samples.

Jacob was raised in a family in which there were eight children. His father was blind and bedridden, due to severe diabetes. His mother earned money by doing housecleaning and laundry for others. Jacob had one older sister who worked in a factory. He wanted to work, but his parents insisted that he go to school and get an education. Except for the youngest two children who were still infants, his five other siblings were sisters. Jacob felt that his mother should not have to work so hard to make ends meet. Periodically, on his way home from school he would walk in the market area and, when vendors had their backs turned, would steal some fruits or vegetables for the family. He would tell his family a story about a friend at school who would bring in some produce to share with others because the father was wealthy.

You meet Jacob at his nursing home, and he tells you this story and others about his stealing. How do you feel about Jacob? Is he someone you feel has values that are different from yours? Can

130

you accept his stealing, based on his lifestyle and circumstances? Are you comfortable being with Jacob and listening to his story?

This scenario also involves stealing. David began to use heroin with his friends when he was seventeen years old. At first, it was just something that was fun to do. Instead of relaxing with alcohol on weekends, he and his friends tried heroin and liked the feeling when they had that momentary high. For the first two months he used just one or two bags on a Saturday night. It cost $20.00. But then David noticed that two bags no longer gave him a high, and he needed three and then four. Then he noticed that if he just used it on Saturday night, when he got up on Sunday he felt sick with flu-like symptoms of sniffles, achy joints, stomach cramps, and diarrhea. They stopped when he bought more heroin and used that. The heroin did not even give him a high. It just prevented him from feeling sick. Now he was "hooked." He needed heroin every day to not feel sick. It now cost $40.00 per day. He used whatever money he had in his bank account. He had a job, but eventually he lost that because he was always taking time off because he felt sick when he couldn't get his heroin.

He began selling his own possessions, then turned to stealing from his family, and finally robbed houses and shoplifted from stores.

You visit David in the hospital and he shares his story of hardship with you. How do you feel about David? Is he someone who has values that are different from yours? Can you accept his stealing, based on his circumstances and lifestyle? Are you comfortable being with David and listening to his story?

Still another scenario might involve a visit to an AIDS patient. He talks to you about the story of his illness and his treatment and why he is hospitalized at this time. He tells you about being a homosexual and how his boyfriend contracted the AIDS virus first. His boyfriend died about six months ago. Before the death, they had lived together, and this patient had taken care of his friend for as long as he could. He is still grieving his friend's death even now and has contracted pneumonia, for which he is presently hospitalized.

How do you feel about this patient? Does he have values that differ from yours? Can you accept that he is ill and grieving? Are you able to listen to his story and thereby help him work his way through his grief?

Or what about this scenario? A patient is hospitalized for an attack of pneumonia, due to AIDS. He contracted the virus around 1980 from a blood transfusion that was given to him when he had surgery after a car accident. At that time, they did not screen blood donations for the AIDS virus. He was unaware he was HIV-positive for about ten years until he started feeling some effects of the disease. He had no other risk factors that could have possibly caused him to contract the virus and thus narrowed it down to the 1980 blood transfusion. He is upset because he is married and has three children, ages eleven, fourteen, and eighteen. He wants to be there to see his children grow up and achieve their hopes and dreams. He wants to attend activities with them now, such as soccer games that his eleven-year-old plays weekly, concerts that his eighteen-year-old daughter performs in, and so forth. His illness forces his wife to work full time, so she is not around to drive the children to their activities. He feels that his disease has robbed his children of the normal, happy life he had hoped to provide.

How do you feel about this patient? Is he someone whose values differ from yours? Are you able to listen to his story and to help him work through his grief?

After discussing scenarios like these, it is important to review the aims of *bikur cholim*, focusing on the volunteer as an active listener and one who enables the patient to sort out and deal with issues pertinent to the current illness or handicap.

Volunteers can then discuss in a group how their values might get in the way of doing this, how they might take certain steps to minimize this from happening, what steps to take, and the ability to decide not to take on a situation in which they feel their values will not allow them to perform *bikur cholim*.

The key purpose of this exercise is to help volunteers assess and recognize potential problem situations; to make them aware of actions they might try to prevent problems, both for the patient and for the volunteer; and to give them permission to say "no" to a situation that they feel unable to handle at this time.

## DEALING WITH THE DEATH
## PROCESS AND GRIEF

An important issue in illness and aging centers around loss and grief. The patient gets a diagnosis and begins treatment. Sometimes the family has a hard time dealing with the diagnosis and tries to shelter the patient from its severity. This prevents the patient from dealing with necessary issues and comprehending the true situation in order to process feelings in a healthy way. If the volunteer replicates the family's actions by being unable to allow the patient to deal with the issues at hand, then stress becomes too great for both the patient and the volunteer. The *bikur cholim* visit is then not allowed to become everything it is capable of being. The patient has no one to help him deal with his stress and sort out his issues. The visitor does not grow from his experience either, and it becomes frustrating as the patient becomes weaker and closer to death and no one talks about it.

In this training, the facilitator will help the volunteer deal with feelings regarding death and illness. Here are some issues that the participant should be asked to reflect on: (1) What is the first death that you can remember? (2) Can you recall some of the emotions you felt at the time? (3) Can you recall the first funeral you attended? (4) What were some of the images of that funeral that you recall? (5) What was your most recent loss and how long ago? (6) Whose death would you have the most difficulty with?

Then give a ten-minute assignment to the volunteers to write their own obituary. What are the things you would wish to be remembered for? How would you sum up your life?

After this assignment, have participants share what they wrote or what it was like to write this assignment.

By choosing to perform *bikur cholim*, we are potentially coming in contact with death as we visit with people who may be facing death. In the American culture we are taught to do just the opposite—to run away from death and to deny it. In denying it, we lose out on the potential enrichment that working through it can bring. By enabling the patients we visit, we help them to enrich their lives in much the same way that writing our obituary in this exercise has helped us to better understand our life and its meaning.

After this exercise, the facilitator might want to close by reading some psalms, such as Psalms 121, Psalms 91, and Psalms 23. These are all used to comfort grievers at the time of a funeral.

## KEEPING MEMBERS INVOLVED AND RECRUITING NEW MEMBERS

Besides the trainings and emotional support, it is also important to find ways to let volunteers know that the work they do is important and needed. There are numerous ways to do this. Part of this recognition has to do with being sensitive to volunteers as people. A smile and a friendly greeting by committee members shows the volunteer he is important. Positive expressions by staff, by the family of the patient, by other volunteers, and by committee members about the work a volunteer does should be given to the volunteer as it happens.

There are other ways to show recognition as well—a birthday card can be sent to the volunteer on his birthday and an anniversary recognition letter sent on the annual date of his volunteer work. Sometimes dinners or informal teas may be offered to the volunteers so they can get together and meet other volunteers. A monthly newsletter listing the happenings and perhaps highlighting one or two different volunteers would be helpful. If a volunteer misses several visits, the *bikur cholim* chairperson should call to find out if he has health problems or mental fatigue regarding his current volunteer situation, which may be too stressful. The *bikur cholim* chairperson should enable the volunteer to cope with these issues. It is also important for the *bikur cholim* chairperson to be available when issues arise that need immediate counseling, and the chairperson should ask for routine feedback regarding how the visit went and what suggestions the visitor might have about how to stimulate still further growth from the process. Use of more experienced volunteers who share their expertise to help train others helps the chairperson and also further illustrates to the experienced volunteer that he has value. Allow experienced volunteers to be buddies to new volunteers. Allow volunteers to take on more responsibilities as they feel more confident of their skills. (For example, a volunteer who originally did group volunteering once a month for Jewish holiday presentations might have met a particular resident whom he would like to visit individually on a weekly basis. Allow him to switch his job duties if you and he feel it will be beneficial and will promote positive growth.) Always defend your volunteers against hostile staff, and try to help such staff persons see the true benefits of using volunteers.

Contact local newspapers to write stories on your volunteer program events and ask them to feature stories using quotes from the volunteers or to actually do full stories on some of their experiences. This is how you can advertise to get new volunteers for your program. Also, speak at synagogues and organization meetings about your program. Try to bring volunteers with you to do the recruiting. Usually, the best way to advertise a program is by word of mouth. It makes the volunteer feel important to be a part of fighting for what he believes is important to him. That's another reason why, after serving as a *bikur cholim* volunteer for close to ten years, I felt that I had to try to do more than just be an individual volunteer. The time came for me to take the next step, which was writing this book to promote the *Bikur Cholim* process. The book could at least show others how to feel more comfortable about trying *bikur cholim* at whatever level is manageable at this time.

In this chapter I also address the issue of a Healing Service. People who go through an illness, families and friends of people who are ill and dying, and also volunteers who visit the ill and dying need some kind of faith and restoration to their souls. A healing service can be very beneficial to them. The last section of this chapter will deal with the role of the rabbi in the *bikur cholim* process. Many *bikur cholim* committees are set up and funded through the local synagogue. That is why I view the rabbis's role as being very important in the founding of the *bikur cholim* committee, in the advertisement of its existence, as the source of referrals to it, and in the continued functioning of the committee, because the rabbi provides a source of healing and restoration to its members.

## THE ROLE OF THE RABBI IN THE *BIKUR CHOLIM* PROCESS

Whenever a family has a member who is ill or dying, they usually turn to their congregation rabbi for advice and guidance. Many rabbis have so many other duties that they often find themselves overworked with commitments. They may make visits to the hospital but find that they are often too pressed for time and cannot stay as long as they would like to. I remember one of my weekly visits to a paralyzed patient, a man with whom I routinely spent forty-five minutes to one hour each week. The rabbi, a hospital chaplain, stopped in to see the patient while I was there. He stood by the man's bed, introduced himself, said he hoped the man would be feeling stronger, and left. He only came to the hospital one or two days a week for a total of about four hours. He obtained a list of all the Jewish patients in the hospital and attempted to make the rounds to see each one. That did not leave him much time to try to carry on a conversation with someone who was paralyzed and who was hard to understand if he did try to speak. How many other people are there who cannot fit into a rabbi's schedule to obtain the quantity of time that might benefit them, and how could this situation be remedied? Of course, the answer is obvious—finding the resources that are available for people from the community to perform *bikur cholim* will take some pressure off the rabbi and will allow the patient to see his Jewish community as a concerned and caring entity.

The hospital where I volunteered had social workers and nurses who were able to discern the benefits of *bikur cholim* for even the critically ill. This is further reinforced by studies reported in two books: *Timeless Healing*, by Dr. Herbert Benson, and *Healing Words*, by Dr. Larry Dossey. They present statistics showing that hospitalized patients who receive prayer and visits and who have religious faith and synagogue or church affiliation live longer after critical and chronic illnesses. Religion seems to ease the spirit, relax the body, and offer a support system.

In New York City the Coordinating Council on Bikur Cholim was established in 1986 by Rabbi Isaac Trainin, an Orthodox rabbi, on his retirement as executive director of religious affairs for UJA (United Jewish Appeal) Federation. *Bikur cholim* is a "forgotten *mitzvah*," according to Trainin, and the purpose of the Coordinating Council on Bikur Cholim is to encourage synagogues to start *bikur cholim*, to provide opportunities for networking, and to train volunteers. This is accomplished through the council's affiliation with the Jewish Board of Family and Children's Services, which in turn is funded by UJA. They run training programs for *bikur cholim* committees in the greater New York area.

Trainin believes that *bikur cholim* is for everybody; even if one does not believe in the lifestyle led by the person who is ill, it is still important that each person, no matter what his lifestyle or values, be entitled to a visit from a member of the Jewish community. This also includes people who are not affiliated with any synagogue.

Trainin also emphasizes the importance of training. Even though some rabbis do not understand, it is important to educate volunteers in order to prevent the disaster of saying the wrong thing and in order to enrich the experience of both the volunteer and the patient. An example of a problem visit is the case of the volunteer who, when told by the patient that he had a certain illness, immediately said to the patient that her brother had died of that disease (from *The Jewish Week, Inc.*, July 16–22 1993).

Rabbi Sholom Stern, president of the Coordinating Council on Bikur Cholim, feels that it is wrong to "professionalize" the *mitzvah* of *bikur cholim* to be just something that rabbis do. Just as in talmudic times spiritual leadership was entrusted to scribes or scholars in the synagogues and schoolhouses, so, too, should the layman share with the rabbi in carrying out the *mitzvah* of *bikur cholim*.

Furthermore, Rabbi Stern states:

> The *mitzvah* of *bikur cholim* is not only an act of kindness, it is a supreme privilege that has been granted to us. To aid one in his or her healing process is to do the holy thing. There is nothing greater. The glory of God is reflected in the majesty of *bikur cholim*.
>
> Those who are privileged to observe the *mitzvah* of *bikur cholim* are a major source of moral energy that affects not only the sick individual, but the spiritual texture of our entire community. (*The Jewish Press*, January 10, 1997, p. 73)

Other rabbis also feel the importance of *bikur cholim* training to get volunteers involved in the process.

Rabbi Nancy Flam and Rabbi Amy Eilberg presented workshops at *Ruach Ami*, the Bay Area Jewish Healing Center in San Francisco, to help train volunteers to perform *Bikur Cholim*. They wrote these ideas in a training manual that I previously mentioned (*Acts of Loving-Kindness: A Training Manual for Bikkur Holim*). There are six training sessions to be used in any way the *bikur cholim* or adult education facilitator feels will be beneficial. It could be for training, for enrichment (refining skills), and/or for refreshment and sustenance for an already formed and ongoing committee.

Rabbi Flam sums up *bikur cholim* in this way: "Being present is what *bikur holim* is all about. By visiting, we hope that the one who is sick feels less isolated, more loved, and more truly in the company of God; our presence should be a vehicle for magnifying the person's feeling that God is near" (p. 25).

Rabbi Joseph Ozarowski, a rabbinic consultant to the National Center for Jewish Healing and author of *To Walk in God's Ways: Jewish Pastoral Perspectives on Illness and Bereavement* (published by Jason Aronson in 1995), sees healing prayers, which are different from normal structured prayers, as helping us call out to God in times of tension and stress. They help relieve anxieties and allow caretakers and visitors to continue to be there for the sick and elderly (*The Outstretched Arm*, Vol. 1, No. 1 [Spring 1998]: 4).

Rabbi Simkha Weintraub, the rabbinic director of the National Center for Jewish Healing in New York City, states that the healing movement combines traditional Jewish *Mi Sheberach* (prayers for the sick) and *bikur cholim* with support groups and healing services in which psalms are read. The Jewish healing movement began in 1991 with a conference that was attended by eleven people. Its aim was to emphasize hope and a sense of community, to address the spiritual needs of Jews confronting illness or death. Rabbi Weintraub's understanding of the spiritual toll that illness takes comes from his own personal experience after having been diagnosed with diabetes and then later with thyroid cancer.

The Jewish Healing Center, which is housed in the offices of the Jewish Board of Family and Children's Services at 120 West 57th Street in New York City, offers a "Sustaining Our Spirits" program. This consists of three spiritual support groups for three different constituencies: support groups for those who are ill, drop-in support groups for Jewish family members of people who are ill, and support groups for Jewish health care professionals working with those who are seriously ill. The aim of these groups is to draw on Jewish tradition and the Jewish community to offer support and hope. The center also offers training sessions for clergy and study sessions about the liturgy of healing and holiday celebrations. Volunteers who work with gravely ill patients often come to center groups to heal and renew their spirits (Steve Lipman, "A Dose of God," *The Jewish Week*, January 24, 1997).

Rabbi Avis Miller, of Adas Israel Congregation in Washington, D.C., asked a congregation member—Jane Handler—to coordinate a symposium on *bikur cholim* to honor the memory of a friend who had recently died of cancer. The symposium's purpose was to show that sharing oneself with a person who is ill and dying helps enhance the limited quality of the patient's life. The symposium was so successful that Rabbi Miller asked Jane and Kim Hetherington to put the material into the booklet, previously mentioned, titled *Give Me Your Hand*. It has become a valuable source book for the history and how-to of *bikur cholim*. A second edition was later published with additional contributions from Rabbi Stuart Kelman and was funded by the Nathan Cummings Foundation, headed by Rabbi Rachel Cowan.

Rabbi Stuart L. Kelman of Congregation Netivot Shalom in Berkeley, California, stated that "after *Shul*, people would go to hospitals and nursing homes to visit." Now it does not happen so frequently. Too few Jews accept this *mitzvah*, and that is why Rabbi Kelman has attempted, with the reissuance of *Give Me Your Hand*, to encourage congregations to sponsor such programs.

Renowned rabbis from all sects of Judaism speak to the importance of participation in *bikur cholim* by members of the Jewish community. Some of these include Rabbi Bradley Artson, whose chapter in his book *It's a Mitzvah!* details how to perform *bikur cholim*, and Rabbi Rachel Cowan and Rabbi Harold Kushner, both of whom lost close loved ones to death. Rabbi Cowan, director of the Nathan Cummings Foundation Jewish Life Program, helped the National Center for Jewish Healing get a grant to start its programs. Cowan saw it as an important aspect in helping Jews find meaning in Judaism. Illness, she feels, is one of the times when a person is most intensely searching for something.

In addition to those persons already cited, I would like to talk about four rabbis who have helped me along my path toward understanding the importance of community participation in *bikur cholim*.

I grew up in the Conservative congregation in Buffalo, New York, where the well-known late Rabbi Isaac Klein, author of *A Guide to Jewish Religious Practice*, was the presiding rabbi. Although *bikur cholim* was not promoted as a community service project for youth groups, it was done by many members of women's groups that were sponsored by the synagogue, such as Sisterhood. The need to advertise for members for a *bikur cholim* society was not as critical then as it is today, because the majority of women of that generation stayed home with their families, and as the children got a little older, the mothers were available to volunteer. I remember with pride how these women of my mother's generation were always available for their families and to perform *mitzvot* like *bikur cholim*. Then there was pride in that kind of *work*, in contrast to the feeling I sense too often in our present generation of putting career first, along with giving less time to the family, which is usually billed as "quality time." Because of the nature of our society today, it may be necessary for women to work because of financial reasons, because of opportunities promoted with the advent of feminism, and because of self-esteem issues. But I still feel that if both men and women and even families give *bikur cholim* a try and make a commitment for a few hours on a regular basis, they could certainly find many benefits for their own well-being. The roots of my passion for *bikur cholim* were set in the congregation and the generation in which I was raised.

Rabbi Steven Moss of B'nai Israel Reform Temple in Oakdale, New York, has served as a chaplain at the Sloan-Kettering Cancer Center, New York Hospital in Manhattan, and at the Southside Hospital in Bay Shore, Long Island. He received recognition in 1994 for years of service as a hospital chaplain. One of his most memorable experiences occurred in 1971 at Sloan-Kettering when he was called to visit a nineteen-year-old man dying of leukemia. Rabbi Moss was the first rabbi to visit him in his three weeks of hospitalization. The young man asked him, "Rabbi, where is the justice in this?" Rabbi Moss replied, "I would be a fool to give you an answer." He then stayed with the young man for eight hours until he died.

Rabbi Moss came to realize from this experience that people want to interact with someone who cares and that just being there is more important than what is being said.

Experiences like this have put into action his belief in the importance of *tikkun olam*, the repairing and bettering of the world.

As a result, his own congregation has a very active *bikur cholim* committee. Also, as president of the Suffolk Jewish Communal Planning Council, he was active in developing, in conjunction with the Coordinating Council on Bikur Cholim of New York, a program for the establishment of *bikur cholim* groups to visit Jewish residents in many nursing and adult care facilities in Suffolk County, Long Island. This was the program that I coordinated by doing the research that was mentioned at the beginning of this chapter.

A third rabbi that I would like to mention is Rabbi Howard Hoffman, spiritual leader of the Conservative synagogue North Shore Jewish Center in Port Jefferson Station, Long Island. Rabbi Hoffman also views the importance of *bikur cholim* as a benefit to both patients and volunteers. As a result, he worked with clergy of other faiths to set up an interfaith training workshop to prepare lay visitors to be effective visitors to the sick. Beginning on January 25, 1993, I attended this eight-week seminar and upon completion accepted a placement at one of the nursing homes where I still continue to volunteer on a weekly basis.

With the support and assistance of Rabbi Hoffman and our synagogue social action committee, we were also able to do a *bikur cholim* training at the synagogue. This occurred a couple of years after that first interfaith training. Although only about six people attended this training, I saw it as beneficial in that there were a couple of placements made in which volunteers were linked up with homes that needed to service their Jewish residents. I believe that this also had a positive effect on the annual *bikur cholim* visit that synagogue members make on Christmas Day to a local hospital to deliver flowers and caring wishes to patients.

The fourth rabbi that I will refer to is Rabbi Adam Fisher, spiritual leader of Temple Isaiah, a Reform congregation in Stony Brook, Long Island. In an article titled "The Rabbinic Role and Practice in Visiting the Sick" (*Journal of Reform Judaism* [Fall 1982]: 43–55), Rabbi Fisher writes that the layman visit shows concern to the patient, provides good cheer, and reduces loneliness. All these things encourage the patient, improve his morale, and reduce feelings of alienation. But the rabbi performs an additional service by providing a spiritual dimension, showing patients how to relate to God in their situation.

I am able to testify that Rabbi Fisher's beliefs are practiced as written. In 1990 when I spent twelve days in the hospital for surgery to remove a benign brain tumor and for subsequent recuperation, I received a visit from him in which he offered a prayer. Throughout the visit and the prayer I felt a sense of peace and comfort, in spite of the fact that my own congregational rabbi at the time did not call or visit.

A recent experience I had that was also a source of comfort to me in my current role as a *bikur cholim* volunteer was attending a Healing Service presented by Rabbi Fisher at his synagogue. Rabbi Fisher and Cantor Michael Tractenberg offer a monthly healing service, which is advertised in the local papers as well as in the temple bulletin and is open to the public. This service has been held for over a year. Sometimes only a half-dozen people come, but people usually come when going through an illness or crisis, and it is important if it can help even one person. When I went, I saw it as an important service to refresh those who are stressed from performing *bikur cholim*; such a service can renew the soul and help the volunteer go on with *bikur cholim*.

*Refuah* (named for the first word of the daily prayer for healing), or healing services, are usually a combination of prayers and meditations.

The service I went to began with the chanting of *hi-nei mah tov u-mah na-im, she-vet achim gam ya-chad* ("How good, how pleasing it is when kindred spirits come together"). This was followed by a blessing for the body and a blessing for the soul, both taken from *Or Chadash*, the *Shabbat* Prayer Book of P'nai or Religious Fellowship.

### Blessing for the Body

Blessed are You, Our God, Who has formed us in wisdom and created within us the spark of life. Each cell does the work of its Creator; each organ's existence is a tribute to God. If but one

143

element of this wondrous structure were to fail in its tasks, we could not stand before You and give thanks for Your sustenance.

*Let us cherish this gift of flesh and blood and honor it as God's creation. Blessed are You, Our God, who performs the miracles of creation and healing.*

## Blessing for the Soul

My God
> The life and soul which You placed within me are pure.
> *You breathed of Yourself into my flesh, creating and forming in me a deep awareness of Your presence.*
> *Praised are You, Ever living God, constantly renewing life within me, with Your breath of love.*

The purpose of the healing is to calm and inspire, to comfort and refresh. More examples of prayers used in this healing service that help to do this are as follows:

## A Litany for Healing (from Numbers 12:13)

When Miriam was sick, her brother Moses prayed: "*Ana, El na la-O,* God, pray, heal her please!" Here is a responsive prayer based on Moses' words:

We pray for those who are now ill.
> *Source of life, we pray: Heal them.*
> We pray for those who are affected by illness, anguish, and pain.
> *Heal them.*
> Grant courage to those whose bodies, holy proof of Your creative goodness, are violated by the pain of illness.
> *Encourage them.*
> Grant strength and compassion to families and friends who give their loving care and support and help to overcome despair.
> *Strengthen them.*

Grant wisdom to those who probe the deepest complexities of Your world as they labor in the search for treatment and cures.
*Inspire them.*

Grant clarity of vision and strength of purpose to the leaders of our institutions and our government. May they be moved to act with justice and compassion and find the courage to overcome fear and hatred.
*Guide them.*

Grant insight to us, that we may understand that whenever death comes, we must accept it—but that before it comes, we must resist it, by prolonging life and making our life worthy as long as it is lived.
*Bless us and heal us all.*

## Prayer for Those Who Help (unsure of exact source)

May the One who blessed our ancestors be a presence to those who provide help for the ill and troubled among us.

May they be filled with fortitude and courage, endowed with sympathy and compassion, as they give strength to those at their side.

May they strive to fight against despair, and continue to find within themselves the will to reach out to those in need.

*And in their love of others, may they know the blessings of community, and the blessing of renewed faith.*

I found the service to be peaceful and comforting. The healing service originally had more appeal among the more liberal wings of Judaism, but now, as it is more often being used and understood, it is appealing to all sects of Judaism. The misconception of a healing service relating to a cure is no longer there. Rabbi Fisher believes . . . "that people today have finally come to understand that prayer and meditation really help deal with the suffering that they feel. Mostly, it's designed to help people feel that they're not alone, that God is present, that God is with them in their sufferings. That, in itself, is a comfort" (*Newsday*, part 2 [May 7, 1996]).

When canvassing ill people about their experiences with *bikur cholim* volunteers, I often heard about patients who complained about having no visitors from the Jewish community. Perhaps these people did not belong to a synagogue and therefore did not have a rabbi to contact about their illness. Perhaps they did belong to a synagogue and they or their families never bothered to contact the rabbi or *bikkur cholim* chairperson. Some hospitals have a Jewish chaplain who comes to visit Jewish patients, and sometimes these rabbis are only there a brief time and may not get to see everyone. Other hospitals or homes do not have a Jewish chaplain involved on a regular basis. Too often, the reason a Jewish patient gets no visitors from the Jewish community is because those who do *bikur cholim* are never contacted.

A potential remedy I would like to suggest for a *bikur cholim* committee is that they contact various local hospitals and homes and call on a regular basis—perhaps weekly—to assess the Jewish population. Then they can instruct their regular volunteers as to where there is a need. The important principle is that every Jew is entitled to a *bikur cholim* visit.

The final chapter will address how a volunteer agency can make its programs effective. Now that all the hard work has been done to obtain volunteers, to inspire them, to teach them how to volunteer effectively, and to make an effective match, there is one new element to consider. How does the volunteer agency keep the people inspired so that they will continue to do the work? In that chapter I will discuss two particular volunteer programs that appear to be very successful in obtaining and retaining volunteers for their programs. I interviewed the directors of volunteers at these programs and obtained information on how they work.

# CHAPTER EIGHT

## EFFECTIVE VOLUNTEER PROGRAMS

Every time I stand outside the door of a hospital room, ready to knock and ask for permission to enter, I feel a certain anxiety as I wonder what situation I will encounter today. Even if the patient is someone I know, I still feel that anxiety. What has happened since my last visit? How can I be of comfort today?

When the nurses or receptionists on the floor greet me with a friendly "hello," or when staff persons say to me, "I'm glad to see you. I have a patient who could use a friendly visit today," then I feel a little more at ease. I feel like I am part of the team.

When I am made to feel that the staff sees me as being in the way and wants no part of me, then I feel as if I should leave. I should not have come to volunteer because my being there is of no value. The excitement that I originally had for trying the challenge of *bikur cholim* slowly fades, and it isn't very difficult to find excuses to justify why I can't come back next time.

When a volunteer assignment involves a task that is too difficult, to the point of becoming frustrating, or too easy, to the point of preventing growth, the volunteer also may not continue to volunteer for very long. For example, the volunteer who agreed to visit Jewish patients during her volunteer hours gave that up very quickly after four weeks passed and the clergyman who was supposed to leave a list of Jewish patients at the front desk never did leave it, even after her repeated calls requesting it. And the volunteer who was asked to work in the admissions office doing filing did not feel that she was doing anything different than she did when she worked as an office clerk.

In order for a volunteer program to keep volunteers, the director must work with the volunteers to make a proper match, must be sure that there is support by the staff for that match, must help the volunteer grow in that match, and must be there to show appreciation and give comfort to the volunteer in a time of stress.

It is important to the success of a volunteer program that the volunteer feels welcome and needed.

In this chapter I will describe two specific volunteer programs that have a high success rate in obtaining and keeping volunteers. These are the Rosalind and Joseph Gurwin Jewish Geriatric Center in Commack, Long Island, and the Harry and Jeanette Weinberg Jewish Terrace in Milwaukee, Wisconsin. Then I will derive some general principles from the workings of these programs to show what volunteer program directors can do to improve their programs, both for recruiting and for keeping volunteers.

## THE ROSALIND AND JOSEPH GURWIN JEWISH GERIATRIC CENTER
## 68 HAUPPAUGE ROAD, COMMACK, NEW YORK, 11725

In the mid-1980s leaders of the Jewish Community in Suffolk County on Long Island joined with UJA—Federation of Jewish Philanthropies to open the first comprehensive geriatric complex east of Queens. The center has beds for three hundred patients for long-term care and short-term rehabilitation and also offers medical adult day care to one hundred persons. The theme of the home is "caring for those who cared for us . . ."

148

This theme is the key factor in the success of the volunteer program run by the center's director of volunteers, Kathleen Donnelly. The first thing that I noticed when Donnelly gave me a tour of the facility was that she knew all the residents and volunteers and greeted them by name. The atmosphere was pleasant and friendly. While waiting in the front lobby to meet Ms. Donnelly, I found it easy to engage in conversation with a resident who was sitting in her wheelchair, busily crocheting a blanket to be raffled off for the holidays. The proceedings would go to purchase materials for recreation at the home. The resident told me about the social programs and also about the fourteen-year-old girl who comes weekly to visit and do crafts with her.

I got the distinct feeling that if I lived nearby, I would choose to visit on a weekly basis at Gurwin because I felt so comfortable being there. I am going to talk about specific areas that the volunteer services at Gurwin use, which seem to make it a successful program.

## Recruiting Volunteers

Gurwin has 200–250 volunteers. The minimum age to volunteer is thirteen. There is no maximum age.

There are obvious ways to recruit volunteers. These include placing ads in newspapers, including community newspapers; Jewish newspapers; synagogue bulletins; organization bulletins such as that of Hadassah, which caters to issues on health and well-being; and school and youth group publications, in order to attract the youth. Mostly, newspaper ads simply state the availability of programs, and they inform people who might have been interested that the programs exist. The ads might actually use success stories in order to propose and promote benefits to the reader.

The next step in recruitment is to appear in public giving speeches that promote the program. In addition to speaking at synagogues and youth groups, Donnelly goes to the Solomon

Schechter Hebrew Day School, located in the Suffolk Jewish Y, which is next door to Gurwin; to Hebrew academies; and to high schools. Some high schools give credits in a community service program, and Gurwin can serve as a field placement.

Also, Ms. Donnelly attended the *bikur cholim* training mentioned in the previous chapter, which was sponsored by the Suffolk Jewish Communal Planning Council. This was a helpful way to advertise her volunteer program to an audience that expressed an interest in *bikur cholim*.

Donnelly also talks about inviting groups in the community to house a meeting at Gurwin and thereby come to see the facility. This may entice them to promote volunteers to come here. Once Suffolk Jewish Communal Planning Council had a dinner meeting that included a tour of the facility.

## Making a Match

When people express an interest in volunteering, the next step is to get them in for an interview. They fill out an application, giving basic information such as name, address, phone number, the days they can volunteer, and the times. It is also important to include on the application a list of special talents the volunteer possesses.

Donnelly states that she really tries to tap into people's skills. In the past, volunteers came once or twice a week and visited with patients in a leisurely manner. Donnelly recognizes that times have changed. People are more busy and don't have a lot of time to spare. If a volunteer commits to coming once a month, that is acceptable. If a person has a specific talent and is willing to come and use that in a project, that, too, is a valuable service. For example, one person originally volunteered as a seamstress, to repair clothing and other items for residents. This provided a much-needed service, and eventually it branched out into something still more valuable. The volunteer organized a sewing circle in which residents got together to sew and chat.

Many volunteers are baby-boomers, who may be retiring from their primary jobs but often are going into second careers. They don't have the luxury of time. But if they are asked to offer a block of time to develop a program that would benefit the residents of the home, they might make a brief commitment. For example, one man volunteered to set up a computer program to help residents with certain tasks.

So the use of volunteers needn't be merely for traditional *bikur cholim* visits. It should be flexible and creative, and who knows when an initial brief commitment might lead to a longer, additional commitment!

A match should be comfortable and not tremendously anxiety-provoking. Sometimes, Donnelly tries to pair an inexperienced volunteer with a trained volunteer so that the new volunteer can learn the ropes and does not have to feel the anxiety of being all alone and perhaps not accepted by the staff or patients. An introduction paves the path. Occasionally, Donnelly also pairs children and parents together. One mother indicated that since her daughter entered her teenage years, they rarely talk, but the joint volunteering really gives them a connection, and they are closer now than they have been for several years.

Donnelly also finds the "grandfriend club" program to be successful. The resident and a youth enter into a relationship like a grandparent and a grandchild.

The volunteer director interviews the volunteer, not only to make the best match but also as a screening to be certain that the person is suited to be a volunteer. For example, Donnelly found that if a potential volunteer had just experienced the death of a relative who was a resident of this particular home, it might be better to give the volunteer approximately six months to grieve. The fresh memories of the loved one's death and his life while at Gurwin may be overwhelming. Also, youths might come here to volunteer because their parents are "forcing" then to come and do a good deed, which might not be in their comfort zone.

Donnelly tries to suggest other kinds of volunteer programs to those persons she feels would be an inappropriate match for

Gurwin. For example, someone who can't handle being around sick people might be better off volunteering at a food pantry, where the job is to package food for poor families.

## Training for *Bikur Cholim*

Students, especially those who are just starting to do *bikur cholim* for the first time, know very little about what to expect. Sensitivity training could be a valuable tool to help make the experience a little easier. It could include sitting in a wheelchair and talking to people who come into the room and remain standing. Is it hard to constantly look up at someone? If food is given to the person in the wheelchair, is it placed on a table that is too high or too far away? What about wearing smeared glasses or being blindfolded? How does it feel to eat and not be able to see what you have to eat? If a volunteer is feeding you, how does it feel if the volunteer talks to others while mechanically feeding you and not telling you what you are eating or asking if you have a preference as to what to eat next? It is a good experience to understand firsthand what the patient could be experiencing. By understanding, the volunteer learns to be sensitive and can thereby make the situation the best it can be.

Along with a simulation of conditions, it might also be beneficial for the volunteer to work with the sense of touch and human contact. Hand-holding or a pat on the back reinforces a connection with people. Rubbing lotion on the dry spots of someone's skin can be a soothing act, too.

It is also helpful to give the volunteer training in regard to dementia, so that he understands that if the patient sometimes acts in a strange way or is offensive, it usually does not mean that the visitor did anything wrong. The volunteer can survive better by knowing that each visit is unique and in some ways unpredictable, because the patient's health and the factors that affect his mental health change daily.

## Support and Follow Up

A volunteer director knows the names of all volunteers, according to Donnelly. She follows up on how the volunteer is doing in regard to the match and is available to answer questions and listen to the concerns the volunteer might have. Observation has to be done carefully. The volunteer should not be made to feel scrutinized, but he should know that a concerned person is available to talk and to listen to him if necessary. If the volunteer does not come to his assignment and does not call in with an explanation, Donnelly tries to phone the volunteer within forty-eight hours to follow up on the situation, to assess whether there might be a problem that needs attention, and to show concern for the volunteer.

The volunteer, although he is not compensated monetarily, is a very important part of the staff. He is given a specific job that he agrees to perform. If he is not performing satisfactorily, the volunteer director tries to guide him and teach him how to improve through training and pairing him with more experienced volunteers. The director is also there to give the volunteer positive feedback about how well he is doing on the job and to recognize him for his contributions. Her aim is to allow the volunteers to see that they make a positive difference by being there.

Donnelly also asks her volunteers for feedback. In order to improve a program, she needs to know what the volunteers get out of volunteering and also what they feel needs to be changed. She recalls with pride one volunteer who proudly said, about his first day of volunteering, "In one day, I never had so many thank-yous as I did today from residents I visited and from staff."

One of the problems Donnelly has to deal with is the way staff persons sometimes treat the volunteer. She tries to help the staff understand the volunteer's importance as a part of the treatment team so that the volunteer is not made to feel in the way. A second problem is grief. A volunteer may have been close to a resident and may come back one week to discover that the resident has died. If Donnelly is aware of the close relationship, she gives

153

the volunteer a call to make him aware of the situation and to tell him about funeral plans in case he might want to attend. She also makes the volunteer aware that there is a support group offered, as well as a social worker and rabbi with whom the volunteer could speak.

Enrichment trainings and recognition ceremonies are also offered annually to volunteers in order to nurture and reward a very important resource.

## HARRY AND JEANETTE WEINBERG JEWISH TERRACE 1414 NORTH PROSPECT AVENUE, MILWAUKEE, WISCONSIN 53202

This facility has a continuum of care, from independent to assisted living. The Jewish Home and Care Center is a 232-bed long- and short-term skilled nursing home. The Helen Bader Center is a unit located within the home and care center for Alzheimer's and other dementia residents. Chai Point is a retirement community with lakefront views. It houses a kosher dining room, convenience store, full-service bank, beauty salon, pharmacy, and parking. In addition, there is a community-based residential facility that helps with additional assistance for dressing, grooming, and nursing. Also on the campus is the Rubenstein Pavillion, which has a banquet hall for meetings and can be rented for special events.

The theme of the Weinberg Jewish Terrace is clearly expressed by this quote on the agency letterhead: "Cast me not off in the time of old age: forsake me not when my strength faileth." The programs developed and run by the community relations coordinator, Kristin Mathisen, are an enactment of this theme. I did not visit this home but spoke at great length to Kristin Mathisen about the program, and she kindly provided me with written statements about community relations programs, which include recruiting, training, and keeping volunteers to service residents, with the result being self-satisfaction and self-fulfillment for many of the volunteers.

Mathisen stresses the three most important components of a successful volunteer program: (1) Recruitment—Good intentions are not enough. The potential volunteer must possess compassion, empathy, and patience, and must be able to deal with death and emotional and spiritual implications in a healthy way. (2) Orientation and Training—Once you have good candidates, Mathisen stresses the importance of teaching them the mission of the program and any concrete skills that they will need to perform the mission. (3) Support for the Volunteer—This would include ongoing training to help them grow with the situation, appropriate counseling staff to be available if they become stressed, and recognizing the volunteers for the important tasks they are performing.

Mathisen sees the residents as everyone's mother and father and stresses the importance of our actions expressing the Fifth Commandment—"Honor thy father and mother."

A written statement is given to potential volunteers from Rabbi Jeffrey Orkin, director of pastoral services. In his statement he talks about the first performance of *bikur cholim* occurring when God visits Abraham shortly after Abraham was circumcised. Nothing was said, but God simply appeared before Abraham and was there for him.

According to Rabbi Orkin,

Volunteers are an important link in the proper care of a resident living in a nursing home—listening to what they have to say, holding their hand, touching their face, smiling at them. It is important to realize that there is no specific right way of visiting the sick. The visit should be a natural reflection of who we are—caring, sensitive with love.

As the Bible has taught us, our visible tangible presence felt by the sick person may be the key to providing quality care to them!

## Recruiting Volunteers

As times have changed, we have lost two very important sources of volunteers we had in the past. These are the parent (usually the mother) who stayed home full-time to raise her children and had some spare time when her children were older and in school and the retiree, who upon retirement had some free time. Now, for many reasons, we often have two-income families. Now retirees retire from one career and go on to pursue a second career.

That is why Mathisen believes that we have to use more than the typical ways to recruit volunteers. Advertising in newspapers and bulletins by describing the successes and benefits of volunteering is, of course, the typical way to recruit, as is speaking in synagogues to the congregation and to Jewish groups such as Sisterhood, which are affiliated with the synagogue. Mathisen also goes to youth groups, religious schools, and public schools to present programs and try to enlist volunteers from that segment of the population as well. Mathisen sees the importance of involving lay leaders by getting them to serve as board members of the home. Some people also come because another volunteer has had a satisfying experience and encourages his friends and family to do *bikur cholim*. Sometimes people volunteer because a family member lives there now, or had lived there in the past and has died. The Weinberg Jewish Terrace has about 125 regular volunteers and some additional sporadic volunteers.

Milwaukee has a central volunteer center where potential volunteers register, giving such information as the kind of work they would like to do and the time and area in which they would be willing to volunteer. This information is computerized and can be accessed by volunteer agencies.

At Marquette University there is a community service course that uses the Weinberg Jewish Terrace as part of its curriculum. The home is the site for five to seven classes per semester, and five to fifteen students at a time are placed there, in a give-and-take relationship.

## Making a Match

When people express an interest in volunteering, they are invited to come for an interview to talk about their skills and talents, to see the possible settings for volunteering, and to discuss potential assignments. Mathisen feels that even if a volunteer can only offer a few hours, he should be encouraged to do that. She stresses the importance of volunteers just being there. Even if a resident is quiet and does not talk, there is a real value to companionship. If we think about how family members might sit together in a room and watch television and not say anything to each other, we can understand that sometimes there is just comfort in knowing that one is not all alone.

In making the match, Mathisen proposes that it is important to set the rules from the onset. She also tries to assess in the interview whether the volunteer has the qualities needed to perform the *bikur cholim* task he has chosen. Trainings, which follow, help the volunteer come to terms with whether his task is something he can handle. If a potential volunteer is still dealing with the recent death of a close loved one, perhaps he is not ready to volunteer in a setting in which residents are critically ill, but he may be able to provide friendship, telephone contact, or help with household errands for someone residing at the Chai Point assisted living retirement community. The key is to get everyone who expresses an interest involved, but at the same time to be sure the match is one that the volunteer is capable of handling and getting satisfaction from, as well as being helpful to the patient.

## Training for *Bikur Cholim*

Training for a candidate for *bikur cholim* always includes a written statement of the goals and objectives of the program and specific tasks that will be expected of the volunteer. There are certain written rules that must be followed, such as confidentiality.

157

The Caring Partners Program at the Jewish Home and Care Center received an award for outstanding Jewish programming at the annual conference of the North American Association of Jewish Homes and Housing for the Aging. It is a hospice-type program that works with the dying patient. Volunteers can get involved with a variety of matches, but material presented here will be about Caring Partners, to show the specifics of how one particular program is handled.

The mission of the Caring Partners Program is clearly written out for the volunteer, and nine objectives are listed. "The mission of Caring Partners is to be of gentle service to residents by offering companionship, support, and comfort in their final days and hours. Our belief is that everyone is entitled to death with dignity and, when desired and possible, in the company of a family member, friend or Caring Person."

Objectives include:

**1.** To be present to listen, to validate, and to comfort.

**2.** To assist the Resident in clarifying and communicating his or her emotional, physical, and spiritual needs and wishes.

**3.** To promote a peaceful, pain-free environment.

**4.** To enhance practices that protect and honor the dignity of the individual.

**5.** To advocate on the Resident's behalf, when necessary.

**6.** To recognize and respond to the needs of the Resident's family.

**7.** To provide ongoing education and team support for Caring Partners volunteers.

**8.** To recruit and train volunteer Caring Partners from the community for the purposes of perpetuating our mission.

**9.** To nurture a diverse, creative, and compassionate working team that fully recognizes that death is a part of life and a natural process to be respectfully embraced and honored.

Through an actual training seminar with multiple speakers from a variety of disciplines, volunteers become educated on the whys and how-to's of carrying out the activities listed on the mission statement. Topics in a recent training included the volunteer director speaking on "Practical Concerns for the Volunteer," a rabbi speaking on "Jewish Perspectives on Dying," a physician speaking on "Physician's Guide: Stages of Dying," a nurse speaking on "The Nurse's Role and Ongoing Care," a psychologist speaking on "Emotional Needs of the Dying/'Taking Care' of the Caring Partner," and a social worker speaking on "Family Support, Confidentiality."

Volunteers are also given a specific list of guidelines concerning the role of the volunteer. It includes a statement that the volunteer can call the volunteer coordinator for support.

Thus, the volunteer becomes a paraprofessional who works with a team of professionals to serve the residents in the best way possible. Job duties are clearly spelled out, and intense training is given to help prepare the paraprofessional for his job.

## Support and Follow Up

Support is there for the paraprofessional at every step of the way. After orientation, the volunteer coordinator follows up with the volunteer to ask about how the placement went. In some placements such as Caring Partners, new volunteers are paired up with more experienced volunteers, and there is buddy-to-buddy mentoring. There are medical doctors and nurses available to the volunteers to answer medical questions. A rabbi is available for spiritual counseling, especially in the case of any grief that might be experienced after the death of a patient. Also, there are volunteer support meetings available to help the grieving process, which is a normal reaction when a good friend dies.

All of these options are listed on an orientation handout that addresses the role of the volunteer. The language is very supportive and recognizes the importance of the volunteer who has selected this position. For example, the first paragraph states:

> You will be assigned to a patient/family as a Hospice volunteer. You will become involved in caring and visiting this family. Your first visit will be difficult. Questions that will be going through your mind are "Will they like me?"; "Will I be able to help?"; "What will I do?" These questions are natural. Just remember at these times of doubting that you have been selected to serve as a Hospice Team Member because people experienced in the field have confidence in YOU! Just "plunge in," taking with you an attitude of openness and receptivity to the needs of the patient/family to whom you have been assigned. They will let you know what they need, and you, in turn, will let them know what you can offer. The relationship will unfold in a natural way. Remember that you can call the Volunteer Coordinator for support/help.

Volunteers are known by name to the director of volunteers. They are encouraged to talk through difficult situations with the proper support people. They are asked to come to ongoing trainings and support groups as needed. They are evaluated quarterly for certain programs and at least annually for others. Monthly luncheon meetings are provided for volunteers to share stories and experiences. Recognition is given to volunteers for their part on the team.

Volunteers are asked for feedback about their *bikur cholim* experiences. Mathisen stated:

> The single most unexpected result of our Caring Partners program was having volunteers report that their own lives, in particular, the spiritual aspects, became more focused and much more precious to them in light of their volunteer work. They became more committed to family and time spent in meaningful exchange, as opposed to, say, mindless recreation. Some experienced a spiritual reawakening, akin to what is often associated with individuals in

the aftermath of tragedy or trauma, only this was born of positive, powerful, REAL contact with another human being.

From studying these two well-recognized volunteer programs, I have derived eighteen general principles that will make a volunteer program effective. I would like to label these the CHAI of a volunteer program.

**1.** Be creative about recruiting volunteers. Use the normal procedures, such as newspaper ads and speeches to synagogues, churches, and service organizations. Use volunteers to speak about their positive experiences.

**2.** Also, tap into the energy and idealism of the younger generation by trying to involve schools, youth groups, Girl Scout and Boy Scout troops, and so forth, in the process. The sick and elderly need to see young people, and they have a lot of expertise and history to share with our youth.

**3.** Hook up with high schools and colleges to offer them an opportunity to give school credits and firsthand experiences in field placements for community service.

**4.** Entice community support. Offer prominent community leaders the chance to be on the Board. Use a community room, theater, or dining hall to invite a community group to have a meeting or meal there. Then give a tour of your facility.

**5.** Don't turn away volunteers who can only offer minimal time to volunteer. Be of the theory that once they begin with a small task, if they like it they may find more time in the future.

**6.** Be creative about tasks for volunteers. Try to assess and use their skills. If you would like to start a creative writing program, perhaps a retired English teacher might volunteer to write the curriculum for one. Use the teacher's talents.

**7.** Assess volunteer skills and try to help people find a task that will not seem too scary and overwhelming but at the same time will provide some satisfaction and growth.

**8.** Outline clearly in writing the rules and expectations of the *bikur cholim* job. Ask the volunteer to sign an acknowledgement that these regulations are something he can follow. Also, get a clear statement from the volunteer regarding days, hours, and times he can volunteer. In other words, get a commitment of some kind from the volunteer. Even though there is no monetary payment, the volunteer is performing a job.

**9.** Treat the volunteer as a paraprofessional and as a team member. If a volunteer is made to feel in the way and unwelcome, he is not likely to continue to volunteer. Speak to staff persons about your concern if they are not courteous to volunteers.

**10.** Provide training to the volunteer so that he understands the principles of how the agency is run and the philosophy of treatment. Give the volunteer a written statement about the philosophy of *bikur cholim* and the mission of the agency.

**11.** Provide training on death and dying so that the volunteer understands some of the issues the patients may be dealing with and knows how to better interact. Also, this can help the volunteer understand the grief process, which he may have to face if the patients with whom he has formed a relationship die.

**12.** Provide support for the volunteer. If it is a new volunteer, he may benefit by being given a buddy who is more experienced in *bikur cholim*. Have the director readily available for support, and also give the volunteer a list of other places he can turn to for advice and support, such as a rabbi who could provide spiritual counseling.

**13.** The volunteer director should know the names of all volunteers and should keep track of how the volunteer assignment is progressing. For example, the director may call a new volunteer on the phone one or two days after the first experience just to be sure the volunteer is not too overwhelmed. If a volunteer stops coming for a period of time, the director should be aware of this and should contact the volunteer regarding his welfare.

**14.** The director should provide regular supervision and evaluation, both to show concern and support for the volunteer and also to verify that the match is acceptable.

**15.** Recognize the importance of the volunteer. There are many creative ways to do this. Examples are an annual luncheon with awards, such as pins that indicate the number of hours volunteered and certificates showing the hours. Send a birthday card to the volunteer. Send holiday cards and provide token holiday gifts, such as a coffee mug, pen, or water bottle with the agency name on it.

**16.** Ask volunteers to speak in public at specific scheduled recruitments about the benefits of *bikur cholim*. Include volunteer statements and pictures in newspaper publicity articles.

**17.** Always be friendly and extend a warm hello to volunteers.

**18.** Ask volunteers for input on how to improve and change programs and use their suggestions to try to improve your program.

# Resource Guide

Association of Jewish Family and Children's Agencies
"Elder Support Network"
3086 State Highway 27, Suite 11
PO Box 248
Kendall Park, NJ 08824
Phone: (800) 634-7346 Fax: (908) 821-0493 Email: ajfca@aol.com
   Helps with referals for frail elderly persons to agencies that pro-
vide a variety of services to keep the elderly at home (home deliv-
ered meals, visitors, transportation, and so on).

Coordinating Council on Bikur Cholim
Rabbi Isaac Trainin, Executive Vice President
c/o Jewish Board of Family and Children's Services
130 East 59th Street, Room 517
New York, NY 10022
Phone: (212) 836-1197 Day Fax: (212) 836-1244; Evening Fax: (212)
   249-7010
   Publishes a directory of *bikur cholim* Resources, coordinates
trainings on *bikur cholim* in the Greater New York City area,

encourages synagogues with *bikur cholim* programs to serve everyone in need, encourages nursing home and homebound visits in addition to hospital visits. Publishes a training manual called *Yad L Yad*.

Jewish Community Centers Association of North America
15 East 26th Street
New York, NY 10010-1579
Phone: (212) 532-4949 Fax: (212) 481-4174 E-mail: info@jcca. org
Central agency for Jewish Community Centers and YM-YWHAs. Relates to *bikur cholim* in that it provides services for hospitalized VA patients through the Jewish Chaplains Council. Publications include *Circle, Briefing,* and *Personnel Reporter*.

National Center for Jewish Healing
c/o JBFCS
120 West 57th Street
New York, NY 10019
Phone: (212) 632-4705
Promotes spiritual healing in the Jewish community. Publishes *The Outstretched Arm*, a quarterly newsletter on healing resources, programs, and experiences; also publishes many resources; runs workshops on healing programs. Has a training manual called *Acts of Loving Kindness*.

National Institute for Jewish Hospice
8723 Alden Drive, Suite S 148
Los Angeles, California 90048
Phone: (800) 446-4448 (213) HOSPICE (California only)
This agency serves as a national Jewish hospice resource center. Has conferences, research, publications, referrals, counseling and guidance, training, and information to patients, families, clergy, caregivers, and volunteers who work with the Jewish terminally ill. Its publication is the *Jewish Hospice Times*.

North American Association of Jewish Homes and Housing for
the Aged
316 Pennsylvania Avenue SE, Suite 402
Washington, DC 20003-1175
Phone: (202) 543-7500 Fax: (202) 543-4090
Helps nonprofit nursing homes and housing programs get together so they can share programs and legislative concerns that
may benefit interests of residents in their long-term care facilities.

Ruach Ami: Bay Area Jewish Healing Center
3330 Geary Blvd., 3rd Floor West
San Francisco, CA 94118
Phone: (415) 750-4197
Fax: (415) 750-4115
Provides individualized Jewish spiritual care for those who are
ill, their loved ones, and the bereaved. Rabbis focus on how Jewish spiritual resources can be used to promote spiritual healing and
wholeness. Also provides training for health care professionals.

Twin Cities Jewish Healing Program
c/o Jewish Family and Children's Service of Minneapolis
1500 South Highway 100, Suite 100
Minneapolis, Minnesota
Phone: (612) 542-4840
Provides and coordinates resources and services that meet the
needs of the Jewish community around experiencing loss, life
challenges, illness, dying, and grief. Does *bikur cholim* training,
coordinates educational programs, and has a resource library.

# READING GUIDE

Adams, Barbara. *Like It Is, Facts about Handicaps from Kids Who Know.* New York: Walker and Co., 1979.

Address, Rabbi Richard F. *The Synagogue as a Caring Community,* Vols. 1-111. Philadelphia: Union of American Hebrew Congregations, Pennsylvania Council, n.d.

Aries, Philippe. *Western Attitude toward Death: From the Middle Ages to the Present,* trans. Patricia M. Ranum. Baltimore: Johns Hopkins University Press, 1974.

Artson, Bradley Shavit. *It's a Mitzvah! Step-By-Step to Jewish Living.* West Orange, NJ/ New York: Behrman House/Rabbinical Assembly, 1995.

Battle, Richard V. *The Volunteer Handbook: How to Organize and Manage a Successful Organization.* Austin, TX: Volunteer Concepts, 1988.

Benjamin, Alfred. *The Helping Interview.* 3rd Ed. Boston: Houghton Mifflin, 1981.

Benson, Herbert, et al. *Timeless Healing.* New York: Simon and Schuster, 1997.

Berrin, Susan, ed. *A Heart of Wisdom.* Woodstock, VT: Jewish Lights, 1997.

Blanchard, Rabbi Tzvi. *Joining Heaven and Earth: Maimonides and the Laws of Bikkur Cholim.* New York: Jewish Healing Center, 1994.

Bletter, Diana. *The Invisible Thread.* Philadelphia: Jewish Publication Society, 1989.

Blue, Rose. *Grandma Didn't Wave Back.* New York: Watts, 1972.

Bockelman, Wilfred. *Finding the Right Words.* Minneapolis: Augsburg Fortress Publications, 1990.

Brammer, Lawrence M. *The Helping Relationship.* 4th Ed. Englewood Cliffs, NJ: Prentice Hall, 1988.

Brenner, Anne. *Mourning and Mitzvah.* Woodstock, VT: Jewish Lights, 1993.

Buxbaum, Yitzhak, *Jewish Spiritual Practices.* Northvale, NJ: Jason Aronson, 1990.

Canfield, Jack, Mark Victor Hansen, Jennifer Read Hawthorne, and Marci Shimoff. *Chicken Soup for the Woman's Soul.* Deerfield Beach, FL: Health Communications, Inc., 1996.

Cardin, Rabbi Nina Beth, Rabbi Nancy Flam, Rabbi Simkha Weintraub. *A Leader's Guide to Services and Prayers of Healing.* New York: National Center for Jewish Healing, 1996.

"Directory of Bikur Cholim Resources," 6th Ed. Coordinating Council on Bikur Cholim, 130 East 59th Street, New York, NY 10022, 1996.

"Directory of Hospital Facilities & Their Services for Jewish Patients in the New York Metropolitan Area," 2nd Ed. Coordinating Council on Bikur Cholim, 130 East 59th Street, New York, NY 10022, 1997.

D'Augelli, Anthony R., Judith Frankel, and Steven J. Danish. *Helping Others.* Monterey, CA: Brooks/Cole Publishing Co., 1981.

Delton, Judy, and Dorothy Tucker. *My Grandma's in a Nursing Home.* Niles, IL: Whitman & Co., 1986.

DOROT. *A Guide for Friendly Visiting.* DOROT, Inc., 171 West 85th Street, New York, NY, n.d.

Dossey, Larry. *Healing Words: The Power of Prayer and the Practice of Medicine.* New York: Harper and Collins, 1995.

Ellis, Susan J., Katherine H. Noyes. *By the People, a History of American Volunteers*. Philadelphia: Energize Press, 1978.

Epstein, Sharon S. "Final Entrance," *Sh'ma*, Vol. 22, No. 425 (January 10, 1992): 37–38.

—— "Is There Meaning to a Brain Tumor?" *The New York Times*, July 22, 1990.

Epstein, Sharon Selib. "Visiting the Sick: Understanding the True Meaning of Mitzvah," *Na'Amat Woman* (May–June 1996): 24–26.

—— "What the Dying Give to the Living," *Chicago Tribune*, December 1992, Section 1.

Erikson, Erik H. *Childhood and Society*. New York: W. W. Norton and Company, 1963.

Fassler, Joan. *Helping Children Cope: Mastering Stress through Books and Stories*. New York: Macmillan Free Press, 1978.

Flam, Rabbi Nancy, Janet Offel, and Rabbi Amy Eilberg. *Acts of Loving-Kindness: A Training Manual for Bikkur Holim*. The National Center for Jewish Healing, New York, n.d.

Flam, Rabbi Nancy, ed. *When the Body Hurts, the Soul Still Longs to Sing*. San Francisco: Jewish Healing Center, 1994.

Frankl, Viktor E. *Man's Search for Meaning*. New York: Washington Square Press, 1998.

—— *The Unheard Cry for Meaning*. New York: Washington Square Press, 1978.

Goldin, Hyman E., trans. *Code of Jewish Law*. Rev. Ed. New York: Hebrew Publishing Co., 1961.

Goldstein, Rabbi Harris R. *Being a Blessing: 54 Ways You Can Help People Living with AIDS*. Los Angeles: Alef Design Group, 1994.

Greenbaum, Avraham. *The Wings of the Sun: Traditional Jewish Healing in Theory and Practice*. Jerusalem: Breslov Research Institute, 1995.

—— *Under the Table and How to Get Up: Jewish Pathways of Spiritual Growth*. Jerusalem: Tsohar, 1991.

Greenbaum, Avraham, ed. and trans. *Garden of the Soul: Rebbe Nachman on Suffering*. Jerusalem: Breslev Research Institute, 1990.

Haber, Perry. *A Guide to Organizing Bikur Cholim Societies in Jewish Communities.* New York: Coordinating Council on Bikur Cholim of Greater New York, 1987.

Hain, Marcia Glaubman. *Twice Chai: A Jewish Road to Recovery.* New York: Bloch Publishing Company, 1991.

Handler, Jane, Kim Hetherington, and Stuart L. Kelman. *Give Me Your Hand: Traditional and Practical Guidance on Visiting the Sick.* 2nd Ed. Berkeley, CA: Congregation Netivot Shalom, 1997.

Hill, Karen. *Helping You Helps Me: A Guide Book for Self-Help Groups.* Ottawa: Canadian Council on Social Development, 1984.

Howe, James. *The Hospital Book.* New York: Crown, 1981.

Jaffe, Hirschel, and James and Marcia Rudin. *Why Me? Why Anyone?* New York: Jason Aronson, 1994.

Jakovits, Immanuel. *Jewish Medical Ethics.* New York: Bloch Publishing, 1959.

Jewish Board of Family and Children's Services. *Volunteer Services to AIDS Clients Training Manual.* New York, n.d.

Jewish Hospice Commission. *A Hospice Guide for Care of Jewish Patients and Families.* Los Angeles: Jewish Federation Council of Greater Los Angeles, 1983.

Kaplan, Aryeh. *Jewish Meditation.* New York: Schocken, 1985.

Katz, Nina Dubler. *"Yad L'Yad": A Training Manual for Bikur Cholim Volunteers.* New York: The Samuel W. and Rose Hurowitz Coordinating Council on Bikur Cholim of Greater New York, n.d.

Klein, Isaac. *A Guide to Jewish Religious Practice.* New York: The Jewish Theological Seminary of America/KTAV Publishing House, Inc., 1979.

Koile, Earl. *Listening as a Way of Becoming.* Waco, TX: Regency Books, 1977.

Kubler-Ross, Elisabeth. *Death: The Final Stage of Growth.* Englewood Cliffs, NJ: Prentice Hall, Inc., 1975.

—— *On Death and Dying.* New York: Macmillan, 1970.

Kushner, Harold S. *When Bad Things Happen to Good People.* New York: Avon, 1997.

Kushner, Lawrence. *God Was in This Place and I, I Did Not Know.* Woodstock, VT: Jewish Lights, 1991.

—— *The Book of Words.* Woodstock, VT: Jewish Lights, 1993.

Lamm, Rabbi Maurice. *The Power of Hope.* New York: Simon and Schuster, 1995.

Levine, Aaron. *How to Perform the Great Mitzvah of Bikur Cholim.* Toronto: Zichron Meier Publications, 1987.

Liss-Levinson, William S. *Hospice and the Synagogue Community.* Prepared for the Synagogue Council of America, National Jewish Hospice Task Force, reprinted in Newsletter No. 13 (Fall 1986), Task Force on Bikur Cholim.

Meyerhoff, Barbara. *Number Our Days.* New York: Simon and Schuster, 1978.

"National Directory of Hospital Facilities & Their Services for Jewish Patients across the United States & Canada." 1st Ed. Coordinating Council on Bikur Cholim, 130 East 59th Street, New York, NY 10022.

Naylor, Harriet H. *Volunteers Today: Finding, Training and Working with Them.* New York: Association Press, 1967.

Nossel, Murray. *Bikur Cholim and Storytelling: A New Approach to Visiting the Sick in Hospitals, Nursing Homes and the Homebound.* The Rabbi Isaac N. Trainin Coordinating Council on Bikur Cholim, New York, n.d.

Olitzsky, Rabbi Kerry M. *100 Blessings Every Day: Daily Twelve Step Recovery Affirmations, Exercises for Personal Growth and Renewal, Reflections on Seasons of the Jewish Year.* Woodstock, VT: Jewish Lights, 1992.

Olitzky, Rabbi Kerry M., and Dr. Stuart Copans. *Twelve Jewish Steps to Recovery.* Woodstock, VT: Jewish Lights, 1994.

Ozarowski, Joseph. *To Walk in God's Way.* Northvale, NJ: Jason Aronson, 1995.

Rabin, Roni. *Six Parts Love.* New York: Charles Scribner's Sons, 1985.

Raphael, Simcha Paull. *Jewish Views of the Afterlife.* Northvale, NJ: Jason Aronson, 1995.

Schur, Rabbi Tzvi G. *Illness and Crisis: Coping the Jewish Way.* National Conference of Synagogue Youth, 1987.

Seicol, Sam. *The Jewish Holiday: A Guide to Caregivers.* Hebrew Rehabilitation Center for Aged, 1200 Centre Street, Roslindale, MA 02131, n.d.

Shapiro, Rami M. *Last Breaths: A Guide to Easing Another's Dying.* Miami: Temple Beth Or, 1993.

—— *Open Hands: A Jewish Guide on Dying, Death and Bereavement.* Miami: Temple Beth Or, 1986.

Stenzel, Anne K., and Helen M. Feeney. *Volunteer Training and Development.* Rev. Ed. New York: Seabury Press, 1976.

Strassfeld, Sharon, Michael, and Strassfeld, eds. *The Third Jewish Catalog.* Philadelphia: The Jewish Publication Society of America, 1980.

Struntz, Karen, and Shari Reville. *Growing Together: An Intergenerational Sourcebook.* Washington, D.C.: AARP/Elvirita Lewis Foundation, 1985.

Summers, Barbara Fortgang. *Community and Responsibility in the Jewish Tradition.* New York: United Synagogue of America, 1978.

Twerski, Rabbi Abraham J. *Living Each Day.* New York: Artscroll, 1992.

—— *Growing Each Day.* New York: Artscroll, 1992.

Waters, Elinor. *Instructor's Guide to Training Mental Health Workers for the Elderly.* Rochester, MI: Continuum Center, 1987.

Weintraub, Simkha, ed. *Healing of Soul, Healing of Body.* Woodstock, VT: Jewish Lights, 1994.

# INDEX

AIDS, 22–23, 51, 59, 60, 91
ALS (Lou Gehrig's disease),
  45–46
Abraham, 11–12
Acceptance, as stage in death
  acceptance, 22
Aging
  issues of, 47
  limitations of, 48
Akiva, Rabbi, 12
Alzheimer's disease, 6, 28, 34
  adult children of parents
    suffering from, 28–29
Anger, as stage in death
  acceptance, 21
Artson, Bradley Shavit, 47, 140
Autonomy versus Shame and
  Doubt, 18
Autopsies, 20
Avoidance mechanisms, 43

Baeck, Leo, 40
Bargaining, as stage in death
  acceptance, 21
Basic Trust versus Basic
  Mistrust, 18, 24
Benson, Dr. Herbert, 137
Berrin, Susan, 47
*Bikur cholim,*
  accessing programs of
    interest, 52–53
  benefits of, 45, 47, 57, 137
  chairperson, 103, 118, 120,
    121, 134–135
  children and, 87–88
  commitment to, 54
  committee, 103, 146
  as company for the sick and
    aged, 1–2, 28–29, 30
  as compassion, 46

do's and don'ts of process, 57,
58–101
as an emulation of God's
ways, 11–12
exploring existing programs,
50–52
family participation in, 8
group, initiating, 101
group participation in, 7–8,
52, 87–88
importance of, 14, 40, 46, 47
as Jewish law, 13–14
lack of meaning of, 39–40
lack of time for, 39
maintaining involvement in,
123–124
meaning of, 35
as means of learning, 8, 17, 24
*mitzvah* of, 11, 15, 123
as aid in maturing, 37
objections to, 4–5
obligation to, 9, 12, 13
performing *mitzvah* of, 56
personal gains from, 9
recipients of, 5, 6, 7
researching, 44–50, 113
roles associated with, 3–4,
5–6
rules and description of tasks
to be performed, 53, 121,
162
societies, 14–15, 52, 96
statistics, 122
teenage involvement in, 88
tour of setting, 53
training, 104

visitor's form, 122
volunteers, 4, 53
women's associations, 15
Blessing for the Body, 143–144
Blessing for the Soul, 144
Blue, Rose, 48
B'nai Israel Reform Temple,
141
Board games, 84–85
Bockelman, Wilfred, 47
Bowlby, John, 38

Canfield, Jack, 83
Caring Partners Program, 158,
160
buddy-to-buddy mentoring,
159
objectives, 158–159
Ceremonies
use of for life events, 48
Chai Point, 154, 157
Chairperson, *bikur cholim*,
administrative, 103, 107–108,
118, 121
clinical, 103–104, 108, 123,
124
Chanina, Rabbi, 13
Chemotherapy, 27–28
Christians and Jews
goodwill between, 89
Christmas, 89
Committee, *bikur cholim*
chairperson, 103, 107–108
expenses of, 106–107
organizing, 104–106
selecting chairperson,
107–108

starting, 103
sponsors, 106–107
Communication
active listening, 67–70
with non-verbal patient, 2
Concentration camps, 40, 44
Congregation Netivot Shalom,
56, 140
Contact, human, 29, 75, 78,
152
Coordinating Council on
Bikur Cholim, 3, 50, 106,
112, 137, 138
of Greater New York, 56, 63,
142
Cowan, R. Rachel, 140
Craft activities, 84

Death
and children, 36–37, 48–49
dealing with, 133–134
denial of, 22
personal fears of, 35–37, 46,
62
preparation for, 18, 19
psychological aspects of, 18
questions about, 36
stages of, 47
stages of acceptance, 21–22, 31
Denial and Isolation, as stage of
death acceptance, 21
Department of Jewish Family
Life Education, 56
Departure from bikur cholim
visit, 90–92, 100
after, 92–95, 100–101

polite ways of, 91, 92
reasons for, 91
Depression, 77
as stage in death acceptance,
21–22
Directory of Bikur Cholim
Resources, 50
Do's and Don'ts of bikur cholim,
58–101
after departure, 58, 92–95,
100–101
departure, 58, 90–92, 100
entering the room, 58, 60–63,
97–98
introduction to recipient of
visit, 58, 60–63
preparation for visit, 58–60,
96–97
review of, 95–101
the visit, 58, 64–90
Donnelly, Kathleen, 149–151,
153
Dorot, 51
Dossey, Dr. Larry, 137
Dying
comforting a person who is,
38
difficulty facing person who
is, 33–35

Ego Integrity versus Despair, 19
Eight ages of man, 18–19
Eilberg, R. Amy, 56, 138
Elazar, Rabbi, 13
Eleazar the Great, Rabbi, 14
Eliezer, Rabbi, 13

Entering room for *bikur cholim* visit, 60–63, 97–98
  respect shown for patient, 60
  respect shown for other visitors, 60–61
Erikson, Erik, 18, 19

Family trees, 85–86
Fisher, R. Adam, 142–143, 145
Flam, R. Nancy, 56, 138
Frankl, Viktor, 40, 44–45
Freud, Sigmund, 18

*Gemilut chasadim*, 12
Generativity versus Stagnation, 19
Grandfriend club, 151
Grief, 153–154
  dealing with, 133–134
  stages of, 29
Group visits
  ideas for, 88–89
Guilt
  feelings associated with the sick and dying, 6–7

Habit, 123–24
Hadassah, 105
Handler, Jane, 46, 56, 139
Hansen, Mark Victor, 83
Harry and Jeanette Weinberg Jewish Terrace, 148, 154–63
Healing service, 135–136, 143, 145
Helen Bader Center, 154
Hetherington, Jane, 140
Hetherington, Kim, 46, 56, 140

Hoffman, R. Howard, 142
Holiday
  programs, 7–8
  sharing, 86–87
Hospital
  discomfort felt in visiting a, 38–39
  questions to consider when selecting for *bikur cholim*, 52

Identity versus Confusion, 19
Illness *See also* Sickness
  and young children, 49
  psychological aspects of, 18
Industry versus Inferiority, 19
Initiative versus Guilt, 19
Introduction to recipient of *bikur cholim* visit, 61
Ishmael, 11–12
Interreligious Affairs of the American Jewish Committee, 20
Intimacy versus Isolation, 19

Jaffe, R. Hirshel, 20–21, 45
Jewish Association for Services to the Aged (JASA), 50
Jewish Board of Family and Children's Services, 56, 137, 139
Jewish community center
  and *bikur cholim* committee, 105
Jewish culture
  given back to shut-ins, 35
Jewish Communal Planning Council, 106

Jewish community
  responsibility to care for ill,
    14
Jewish Family Services, 50, 105
Jewish Healing Exchange, 50
Jewish Home and Care Center,
  The, 154, 158
Jews and Christians
  goodwill between, 89

Katz, Jonathan, 55
Katz, Nina Dubler, 55
Kelman, R. Stuart, 46, 56, 140
Klein, R. Isaac, 20, 140
Kozberg, Cary, 48
Kubler-Ross, Elisabeth, 21, 22,
  29, 68
Kushner, R. Harold, 140

Letter writing, 84
Leukemia, 45
Life
  after death in Judaism, 20
  stages of, 9, 18, 20, 35
  value of goals in, 40
Listening, 4, 38, 62, 63, 68
  active, 67-70, 71, 86
  effective, 128-129
  importance of, 27
  patience involved with, 75
  and personal judgments, 129
  objective, 65
Litany for Healing, A, 144-145
Logotherapy, 44-45
  as aid in performing *bikur
    cholim*, 45

Maimonides, 13
Marquette University, 156
Mathisen, Kristin, 154-156, 160
Miller, R. Avis, 139-140
*Mi Sheberach*, 79, 80, 93, 139
*Mitzvah*,
  meaning of, 3, 11
  personal gains from, 3
Moss, R. Steven, 141

*Nashim zadkaniyyot*, 15
Nathan Cummings
  Foundation, 140
  Jewish Life Program, 140
National Center for Jewish
  Healing, 56, 139, 140
Nonverbal cues, 61
North American Association
  of Jewish Homes and
  Housing for the Aging, 158
North American Jewish Data
  bank
  statistics, 47
North Shore Jewish Center, 39,
  89, 142
Nossel, Murray, 63

Offel, Janet, 56
Organ donation, 20
Organization for
  Rehabilitation Through
  Training (ORT), 105
Orkin, R. Jeffrey, 155
Ozarowski, R. Joseph, 139

Patient
  activities to do for the, 83-84

activities to do with the, 84–85

benefits of volunteer visits, 104

confidentiality of, 94–95, 121

over-involvement with, 93

Pet visits, 89–90

Posture of involvement, 63, 64

Prayer, 80–82

and the *Siddur*, 81

statistics supporting benefits, 137

Prayer for Those Who Help, 145

Prejudice, 59, 62, 91

Preparation for *bikur cholim* visit, 58–60, 96–97

comfort issues, 58, 59

conversation openers, 59–60

dressing for, 59

discovering prejudices, 59

Psalms 23, 81

Questionnaire to assess need for *bikur cholim* training, 108–109

Rabbi

and *bikur cholim* duties, 104, 142–43

organizing *bikur cholim* committee in synagogue, 105

role in *bikur cholim* process, 136–43

Rabin, Roni, 45

READY process, 43–54

Recruiting volunteers, 101, 113–118, 135, 149–50, 155, 156

*Refuah*, 143

Response skills

door openers, 70–71

minimal encouragers, 71–72

open-ended questions, 72–74

paraphrasing, 74–75, 76

reflecting back feelings, 76–77

silence, 78–79

Rosalind and Joseph Gurwin Jewish Geriatric Center, 148–54

Rosenstreich, Vickie, 55

Rubenstein Pavillion, 154

Rudin, R. James, 20, 45

Rudin, Marcia, 20, 45

*Sefer Hasidim*, 14

Seminar

advertising, 113–15, 116, 135

news release, 115–16

Sick

comforting the, 64

fears about visiting, 33–41

guide to visiting the, 46–47

limitations of being, 127–128

obligation to rich and poor, 14

visitors to, 2, 13

Sickness

and children, 23, 25

denial of, 30

difficulty facing patient of, 33–35

general rules for coping with, 30
honesty about, 30
and infants, 23–24
and pre-adolescents, 26
personal fears of, 35–37, 62
questions associated with, 30
support of patients of, 30
and teenagers, 26
and toddlers, 23–24
uncertainty associated with, 30
Skills
assessment, 161
fine-tuning to meet situation, 130
learning *bikur cholim*, 55–101
matching to meet *bikur cholim* needs, 113, 117–118, 119–121, 122–123, 148, 150–152, 157
tapping into people's, 150
Sloan-Kettering Cancer Center, 141
Societies
*bikur cholim*, 14–15, 52
influence of Spanish Jews, 14
Solomon Schechter Hebrew Day School, 150
Sponsors for *bikur cholim*
need for, 106–107
Stern, Rabbi Sholom, 138
Story
facilitating telling of, 65
importance of, 63
as means of communication, 2

as means of sharing emotions, 6
as means of teaching others, 4, 62
responses to patient's, 70
uniqueness of each, 69–70
Storytelling, 61–62
Stovich, Dr. Raymond, 68
Stress
negative, 94
positive, 94
Suffolk Jewish Communal Planning Council, 108–110, 112, 113, 142, 150
survey, 108–113
training, 113
Support groups, 139
Surveys, 7
Survival
purpose in, 44

Talmud
references to *bikur cholim* in, 12–13
Temple Adas Israel
symposium at, 56
Temple Isaiah, 142
*Tikkun olam*, 12, 141
Torah Healing Tradition, 50
Touch, 82–83, 152
importance of, 29, 38, 47, 83
Tractenberg, Michael, 143
Trainin, R. Isaac, 3, 112, 137
Training for *bikur cholim*, 157–159, 162
anecdotes, use of, 127–130

on dementia, 152
on death, 133–134
importance of, 137–138
role playing, 125–126, 127,
128–129
sample sessions, 124–136
sensitivity, 152
using scenarios, 130–132
Transplants, 20

UJA-Federation of Jewish
Philanthropies, 148
United Jewish Appeal
Federation (UJA), 137, 148

Visit, the, 98–100
position of involvement, 64
reflecting on, 92–93
statistics supporting benefits,
137
Visitors
Distractions, 63
effective, 35
Volunteer Programs, 147–163
general principles for
effectiveness, 161
Volunteers
advertising for, 115–117, 141
affirmation of patient needs,
66
application form, 119–120
appropriate conversation for,
64–66
appropriate seating for, 63
buddy system, 123
comfort level of, 39, 51
community support, 161

and confidentiality, 94–95,
157
difficulty understanding
patient, 75
director of, 53, 153, 162–163
effective, 126–127
fears, training to address,
124–125
fears of ineffectiveness, 37–38
feedback from, 153, 160
focus on patient, 66–67
frustrations encountered,
147–148
group, 7–8, 87–88
guidelines, 159
interview for, 120, 121,
150–151, 157
keeping, 101, 123–124, 148
monthly support meetings,
123
monthly training meetings,
124
need for Jewish, 106
orientation, 155, 160
pacing of acceptance of role
as, 5
as paraprofessional, 159, 162
personal rewards achieved by,
56
prayer offered by, 79–80
questions considered by, 64
reasons to, 95–96
recognition of, 134–135, 160,
163
recruiting, 101, 113–118, 135,
149–150, 155, 156, 161,
163

role of, 160
stress, 94
support groups for, 93, 154, 155
survey to assess need for, 110
as trainers, 135
training of, 55, 104, 106, 111–112, 155, 157–59, 162

treatment by facility staff personnel, 153

Weintraub, R. Simkha, 139
World Wide Web
as source for research, 49–50

Yochanan, Rabbi, 13

# ABOUT THE AUTHOR

Sharon Selib Epstein is a psychiatric social worker and a New York State certified social worker. She is currently employed by a county health agency and works with those who have alcohol and drug problems. Additionally, she has had a variety of experiences in agencies dealing with mental health, family therapy, and adoption services. She has been an active volunteer in such places as hospitals, nursing homes, and in Jewish organizations. She was a Girl Scout leader for eight years.

Ms. Epstein organized *bikur cholim* training in her community. She has written numerous articles on social issues, including a column for several years for a national magazine on marriage counseling and many articles on the subject of visiting the sick.

Ms. Epstein is married, and she and her husband Larry have four children, Michael, Elana, Rachel, and Lisa.